MW01195597

Scripture References:

Epigraph

The Ordinary Man

By Robert Service

If you and I should chance to meet,

I guess you wouldn't care;

I'm sure you'd pass me in the street

As if I wasn't there.

You'd never look me in the face,

My modest mug to scan,

Because I'm just a commonplace

And Ordinary Man.

But then, it may be, you are too

A guy of every day,

Who does the job he's told to do

And takes the wife his pay;

Who makes a home and kids his care,

And works with pick or pen...

Why, Pal, I guess we're just a pair

Of Ordinary Men.

We plug away and make no fuss,

Our feats are never crowned;

And yet, it's common coves like us

Who make the world go round.

And as we steer a steady course

By God's predestined plan,

Hats off to that almighty Force:

The Ordinary Man.

*The members of the council were amazed when they saw the boldness of Peter and John, for they could see that they were "**ORDINARY**" men with no special training in the Scriptures. They also recognized them as men who had been with Jesus."*

Acts of the Apostles 4:13 NLT

TABLE OF CONTENTS

Introduction

ORDINARY

An Ordinary Man's Experiences With God

This is the beginning of a book of stories, my stories. Stories about me, an ordinary man. They are true stories, at least to the best of my recollection. I hope you or my children, or grandchildren, or great-grandchildren enjoy them. I know that I would like to have known my dad a little better. I barely knew my grandfathers. Don't have a clue what or how my great grandfathers thought. Did they have adventures or stories about their experiences with God?

These stories are my testimony. It is my most sincere hope that they bring glory to God. I so hope they encourage, comfort or inspire you to believe Him and come to know Him more.

God, the greatest author, has placed a story in each of us. He sees the finished product. As an ordinary man, I am, of course, a work in progress. I once heard a preacher say, "You see the glory, but you don't know the story." He means you see the good part not the struggles or the dark nights of weeping and tears. We all have them. I have had my dark nights of the soul. Trust me, I have had my share. These stories are more about answered prayer and experiencing God's deliverance and victory.

To me life is an adventure, at least from my perspective. Maybe that's why I seem to have more adventures than the average Joe. Maybe I see life through the eyes of an adventurer. I love to take risks. In my own mind, I think of myself as cautiously aggressive. As I have gotten older and hopefully more mature, I like to think the risks have become more calculated.

Well now, let's see…which story first? Usually in conversation, I tell a story when the other person prompts a thought or memory of an experience of mine that just might help get my point across or illustrate a lesson, especially a lesson about God. He's the big story.

So, I guess the first story is called, "Lord, Should I Write This Book?" Then the story of "Johnny Cash the Dog." After these, the stories are in chronological order. I think you'll see my progression and growth in faith. Hang in there, God Lovers, Chapter 15 is where the God stories start. My hope is your faith will grow as well.

Chapter One

Lord, Should I Write This Book?

One day I was sitting in my pickup truck in a deserted parking lot thinking about this book that I had started to write. I was wondering if I should finish the book.

I looked out through the windshield at the open sky. With my eyes open, as is my custom, I prayed this prayer: "Lord I don't want to dis (disrespect) you by writing a book that is supposed to be about you, but it is really about me and my big ego. Should I write this book?"

And just as I finished the prayer, the radio came on. A man's voice said loud and clear, "I can't believe how much I've been reading. Why, I have read so many books in the past year. If books were to appreciate in worth, I'm gonna be a millionaire!" He said, "I go to libraries, yard sales and to new and used bookstores looking for a book. I'm looking for a certain book, but I can't find it. What I really want to find is a book about an ordinary man's experiences with God." And then the voice was gone, and the radio was off.

I don't have a clue as to what station it was or who the man was, but I do believe it was the Lord speaking confirmation to me. That's what this book is about. It's a testimony of my life and the stories are about my experiences with God. I believe, that if you call to God, He will answer.

So I titled this book: Ordinary - An Ordinary Man's

Experiences With God.

Chapter Two

Johnny Cash – The Dog From God

This is the story of Johnny Cash. Johnny Cash the dog, that is. How I came to be his man. How he came to be my dog. My dog? Sometimes I think we say, "we own something", but God laughs.

The story starts in November 2016. Location: backwoods South Alabama. My friend Russell and I were hunting deer. I was using a compound bow and Russell was using a crossbow. Russell was new to hunting and this was his first time to use a crossbow. I was helping Russell to get his first deer.

Russell was not quite as accurate as I wanted him to be. He had not perfected the discipline of practice and therefore the art of accuracy. I have a saying that I got from somebody wiser. The saying goes, "It's either discipline or regret." On this particular fall day, we were both regretting that Russell had wounded a deer and we couldn't find him. We tracked the deer for 200 yards but finally lost the blood trail. We went back to the truck that we had parked in an open pasture.

It was a beautiful blue bird day. It was crisp and cool, but I was more than a little frustrated. I said in a somewhat agitated voice, "Russell, we need a dog to trail a wounded deer." I said, "We need a Catahoula."

He said, "What is a Catahoula?" I told him that a Catahoula is the Louisiana state dog. They have been breeding Catahoulas for over 200 years. And that when I was a boy, I used them to hunt cows in the swamps of south Florida. That they were the smartest dogs I had ever known. I knew I could train one to trail a wounded deer.

I said, "Russell, I know you don't believe like I do, but look up into the blue sky and keep your eyes open while I pray. Please agree with my prayer." I looked up into the blue sky also and prayed, "Father, I'm asking you for a Catahoula. To please me and open Russell's eyes to you. In Jesus Name, Amen."

I said, "Now, Russell, we are going to put feet to our prayer."
He said, "What does that mean?"
I said, "Get in the truck."
"Where are we going?"
"We are going to go take a ride in the truck and I'm going to stop at the first house out here in the country. We will go to the door and ask the person that comes to the door if they would consider me giving them $50 a month plus expenses to keep a dog."
You see, I knew my wife did not want to keep a dog at our house, definitely not inside. Where I live on the water, it is so pristinely manicured I didn't want a dog to tear up my backyard. So, I needed a place to keep a dog near my hunting lease in South Alabama.

So, Russell and I got in the truck and drove out to the hard road. After driving a couple of miles, we came to a house with some chain-link kennels behind it. We couldn't see any dogs, but we heard some barking. Russell and I went up to the door and knocked. A lady came to the door.

I said, Ma'am, would you consider keeping a dog for $50 a month plus expenses?"

She said, "I couldn't do that, I breed dogs."

"What kind of dogs?" I asked.

"Catahoulas."

When I looked at Russell his eyes got big and he looked like he was startled. Then we both smiled.

I said, "Do you have one?"

She said, "I have a male, six months old and his name is Johnny. His registered name is Johnny Cash." That was music to my ears and thrilled my soul. It was love at first sight.

I knew right away that he was the dog of my dreams, the dog I always wanted. I just loved the way he looked. I still do. He is perfect to me.

When I took him home, my wife, Debbie, fell in love with him. We keep him at home. Thank you, Lord!

I put my cheek on his cheek and said, "If you'll be my dog, I'll be your man."

It was a relationship made in heaven. That's why I call him my dog from God. I believe with all my heart that God gave him to me. That's the story of Johnny Cash. When you see him on Facebook, I hope you'll feel like you know him.

Oh, and as for the opening of Russell's eyes... Well, he told me he found a Bible the other day at a used bookstore. He said he can't put it down and he has decided that he believes God wants him to serve Him with all his heart.

"Take delight in the LORD, and he will give you your heart's desires." Psalms 37:4 NLT

Chapter Three

First Snake: Overcoming Fear

This story takes place when I was eight years old. My dad always had a hunting camp. The camps were originally in the Big Cypress near the Everglades; one of them actually bordered the Seminole Indian reservation. However, this story takes place at our last hunting camp, which was further north and was a total of thirty thousand acres that bordered Myakka State Park. It was an amazing hunting camp. We built the camp alongside an old canal. It looked like a creek because there were large oak trees on the canal, so the canal must have been dug many years earlier.

We built the camp house similar to the one down in the Big Cypress. It was a long rectangular building that was built up off the ground. It had plywood floors with two main rooms that were divided by a hallway in the middle going to a bathroom. There were four bunks in each of the main rooms, with a tin roof and tin 2' by 10' sheet sides that ran horizontally. About head-high on the outside or bunk-high on the inside, one of the rows of horizontal tin was just nailed at the top. We would fold it and prop it up with long two-by-fours. There was a gap at the top that was screened in. Air came in on all sides. It was fairly cool, even in the summertime. It could be very cold on some winter nights. Instead of having steps, we had a four-by-eight, marine-grade, three-quarter inch plywood ramp that we walked up.

If you came out of the camp house and went about a hundred feet, we had a kitchen that was a 30'x 20' room. It had a tin roof and screened sides all around. In the center of what we called our kitchen, we had a big plywood table made of four-by-eight marine plywood for a tabletop, with benches on either side. We had a big icebox and a gas stove.

We had water from a well and electricity was provided by an unusual generator. It was a diesel, an old "one-cylinder" generator that came from a hospital down in Fort Myers, Florida. One of the camp members was on the hospital board in Lee County, and when they retired this old generator because it was so old-fashioned, we took it up to the camp. It was just an unusual generator. We had it insulated and away from the camp by probably a hundred yards, but it would sound so unusual and loud, making a sound like "Womp Womp Womp Womp Womp…"

Well one morning, I was sitting with my dad and some other men in the kitchen on the benches around that big plywood table. Somebody looked up, and there was a huge rattlesnake crawling across the camp yard. It actually crawled across the ramp we used to walk up into the camp house. It didn't go up the ramp, but it crawled across the bottom of it. We all saw it, and my dad did an unusual thing. He turned to me, an eight-year-old, and said, "John, take that shovel and kill that rattlesnake."

For most dads to do that it would be highly unusual. You would think about shooting the rattlesnake, but to send your eight-year-old son to kill a six-foot rattlesnake, it could be deadly. I'm sure if my mother had been there that would have never happened. But I think my dad somehow instinctively knew that it would be a point in my life for building my own strength and not having fear. He later called it the making of a man.

I was plenty afraid, but I didn't show it. Some kids might have said, "No, Daddy!"

But you didn't know my dad. You'll hear more about him in some other stories. He was a very unusual man. He was a big man, and he was a scary man. He never showed any weakness. He never fraternized with people he worked with, and even with me he never showed much weakness. He was also a hasty man; he was quick. Sometimes he could be angry -- maybe too angry with animals -- but he always treated me very fairly. So, when he told me to kill that snake, there was no question whether I was going to do it.

I took the shovel, which didn't have a very long handle, especially for an eight-year-old boy, and I went up to the snake. I was afraid that maybe the snake would strike. I've heard they strike the length of their body, but I think they can really only strike about half the length of their body. Still, that was three feet long and my shovel handle was at the most four feet long. But because I was, to a measure an athlete and a baseball player, it wasn't too hard for me to whack that snake on the head and kill it.

Then my dad gave me a lesson that I pass on to whoever reads this. With a rattlesnake, you never pick him up by the tail if he still has his head on because his natural reflex is to swing around and make a strike at whatever has his tail. Even though the reptile is dead, his body will reflex and strike. If he sticks you with a fang, the force of the strike presses against a poisonous sack in the roof of their mouth. So, if he strikes you, even if he's dead, he can impart venom and kill you.

My dad quickly said, "Cut his head off." So, we cut his head off. That's the story of my first snake, and one of my first times of learning not to have fear.

Fear is not in God's will for your life. Over three hundred and sixty times He says in His Word, "Fear not." He says, "Be of good courage." Of course, use wisdom, be concerned of danger, but don't be afraid. Be strong in the power of the Lord's might. Be courageous! Be a man! A man of God!

"So do not fear, for I am with you; do not be dismayed, for I am your God. I will strengthen you and help you; I will uphold you with my righteous right hand." Isaiah 41:10 NIV

Chapter Four

"Mike and the Barking Pig"

When I was a boy, my family would take a vacation every summer. When I was ten years old, we were vacationing and traveling through Tennessee. We looked over on the side of the road and saw a sign that said, "Bird Dogs for Sale." To a lot of families that wouldn't mean anything, but when my dad and I saw that sign, our tails started wagging. When a bird dog gets birdie, he smells birds and his tail starts wagging fast. Some of you will understand that; some of you won't.

At any rate, my dad and I got very excited. We always kept about a dozen bird dogs in some kennels in south Florida. We did a lot of bird hunting back then. By bird hunting, I mean quail hunting. There was so much territory to hunt quail where we lived in South Florida.

We had woods and cattle pastures that had a lot of quail in it, and we hunted a lot of other land that was called open land. There was an open range where we had our cattle operation, and every so often there would be a cow drive that would go by there. The cows would be strung out for a mile. The lead cow had a bell around her neck, and the other cows would follow her. This is what we call old Florida. There were few fences at that time when I was a boy. Now everything is fenced, and most of it is subdivisions and golf courses.

Well, we loved to bird hunt. We had a saying that how much you could *bird* hunt wasn't about how much land you had or how many quail there were, but about how many dogs you had. This was because there was plenty of bird hunting territory and plenty of birds. What you didn't have was enough dogs and time.

We had a big Jeep with a big dog box. Two men could ride in the regular seats and us boys would sit up on the top seat on the box and watch the dogs. The dog box would hold about eight dogs, and we had cages on the side of the box that would hold two more on each side. We might take ten dogs hunting.

So, we were definitely serious bird hunters and when we saw that sign that said, "Bird Dogs for Sale," on that vacation in Tennessee, that's why we got excited. My dad made a quick u-turn and pulled up to the country farmhouse. Standing out by a set of dog pens, we met the dog's owner. He showed us a setter bitch that had six or eight puppies that were half English Pointer and half English Setter. Boy, we would have liked to have her because the owner said she was really birdie and would really hold point. However, the pups were just too young. But there was also a big male bird dog there that had a big old head. The owner said he was the best he ever owned, and his name was Mike.

Mike was an English Pointer, a big black and white spotted pointer. He was a beautiful dog and the guy claimed he could really point a quail. So, my dad said, "I wonder if we could stick that dog in the back of the station wagon, John." I exclaimed, "Yes sir!" Before he got the words out of his mouth my older high-browed sister declared there was no way she was gonna ride all the way back to Florida with a stinky dog. It was all I could do to not call my sister a few choice names, but I instinctively knew it could blow the deal. So, I wisely held my peace. Instead I made a beeline to my mom before she could speak and jumped in her lap and sweetly said, "Mom, you know how much I love you. I really want this dog, Mom. If you'll let me have him, I'll feed him and bathe him and totally take care of him. Please, Mom!"

Sure enough, I still don't know how my dad talked my mother and my sisters into it, but next news you know, we are heading back home from Tennessee and that's a long way from South Florida. So, we put old Mike in the back of Mom's station wagon, and it was a long trip. That dog passed so much gas. He kind of became infamous with my mom.

After we got back home, we took Mike out for a ride in the Jeep. Wouldn't you know it, one of the very first things he did made him famous. We were in an open Jeep and he was riding in the back with no dog box. We stopped at a gate in a wide-open palmetto prairie. When I got up to open the gate, I noticed Mike became very rigid and stiff, he was pointing in the jeep. My dad said, "What the hell, that dog's pointing." When we let him jump out of the back of the truck, he just stopped on the ground and pointed again. Sure enough, we flushed out a big covey of quail. We were very impressed that Mike had pointed quail out of the back of the Jeep. First impressions are lasting impressions. It turned out he was a great dog for a lot of years.

The story really begins when we were bird hunting one day with Mike and suddenly, we got into a bunch of hogs. On this particular hunting lease, which was a huge hunting lease (30,000 acres that bordered Myakka State Park), there were lots and lots of hogs. They are called Feral Swine; they're wild hogs. Hogs like that were liable to hurt a bird dog, so normally you wouldn't want your bird dog to get into it with any hogs. But it just so happened there were a bunch of little pigs there with a sow, and next thing you know, we saw Mike come running up to us with a baby pig in his mouth. He was holding him lightly; he wasn't chewing on him. Mike had a "soft mouth" from gently carrying quail. We took the pig out of his mouth, and by this time the rest of the hogs had run off. I said, "Dad, can we keep him? Can we try to raise him on a bottle?" Dad said, "Let's hope he lives."

So, we took him home and started giving him bottles of milk. Pretty soon he got a little too big for the house, so we took him out and put him in one of the dog pens out at my dad's rock plant.

At the rock quarry there was a phenomenon that would happen every day at four o'clock: we would shoot dynamite to blast the rock that would then be dug for the rock plant. All day long, Sherrill, the dynamite man, would load the dynamite in the holes, and then he would shoot it. It would make a very, very loud noise, as you can imagine when dynamite explodes. It is a blast. So, at four o'clock, on the dot, when that big blast would go off every day, those dogs would come rushing down out of their boxes. The boxes were about four feet in the air, and about 4 x 4 cube with hay in it. Then there was a ramp that would come down to the concrete, and there was dog wire on the top and on the sides of the pen. As you can picture, these dogs would go up a ramp to get into their doghouse. At four o'clock every day they would come running down after that dynamite blast and they would sit at the base of their pen. They would all bark, bark, and bark. Well, it was the funniest thing. That hog grew up from a little pig out there with those dogs, and he thought he was a dog growing up. He would come running out, down that ramp, and one day that ramp finally broke. But at four o'clock every day you would see that hog—he'd be sitting on his tail—sitting, and when that dynamite would blast, he'd be barking. He sounded just like a dog; he'd go, "Arf, arf, arf, arf, arf!!!"

So that's the story about Mike and the Barking Pig.

God knows I love dogs.

Chapter Five

My First Job

During the summer when I was fourteen years old, my dad wanted me to go work at his rock quarry. He decided that I was going to be an oiler on a Manitowoc dragline. A dragline is a big machine that was on tracks. It had a long boom and a cable that would run from inside the main house of the dragline, up over the boom and down, and then there was a bucket. This particular bucket was about an eight-yard bucket —that means about how much the bucket would hold.

The bucket was let down by releasing the top cable and drug in by the bottom cable, and it would fill up full of—in this case—rock that had been dynamited under the water. Then the operator would use the lift cable in combination with the drag cable, and by swinging the boom he could put the bucket wherever he wanted. Then he would release the drag cable and the bucket would dump its' load.

On this particular dragline there was an old man named Cassidy. I'm sure he's dead now; he was fairly old at that time. He was an excellent dragline operator, probably one of the best my dad had ever hired. Cassidy would load the portable crusher with that bucket, meaning he would dig, put it out there, drag and fill the bucket, lift it up and swing it over, and dump it in the portable crusher.

There was a man named Art, who sat on top and next to that portable crusher with just a piece of plywood over him to give him shade. He was there so that when boulders hung up in the portable crusher, he could figure out a way to put a cable around the boulder and Cassidy would lift the boulder back up out of there. But it was extremely dangerous because one slight miss of the operation and you could kill Art, sitting there on the side of that portable crusher. Can you imagine sitting there? That portable crusher was so loud, with rock chips flying everywhere, and Art would sit there for ten hours a day. It's no wonder Art didn't hear very well, or me; we had no ear protection. I was working as an oiler and was in charge of keeping everything greased and keeping the proper oil levels, and keeping the moving parts clean as well.

I'm not sure why Cassidy was so grouchy, and halfway mean. He kept running off the previous oilers. My dad would hire one, and they just could not take Cassidy being so mean and grouchy. My dad thought he'd fix both of us. My dad was part owner of the company and general manager and president, and Cassidy really respected my dad. My dad also respected Cassidy. Dad put me there so that perhaps I'd grow up. I think he wanted me to learn about heavy equipment, and to become a man.

Cassidy was, at first, all smiles to me for my dad's sake. They were all afraid of my dad. When I got on the dragline, Cassidy began to show me around. He gave me a type of a mop, and the mop had a wooden handle about fourteen or sixteen inches long. On the end of it was a real fuzzy piece of cotton mop. If you were to dip that in soapy water (or as it was in this case, diesel fuel), it would, of course, not be all fuzzy. It wasn't like a regular mop, the kind that has cords that you use to mop the floor. But this was brand new and all fuzzy. So, I put the mop handle in my back pocket. The idea was that we would dip it in diesel fuel and bathe all the gears and the different parts of the machine. That kept the gears from getting dry; it was lubrication. We also used different oils for different things. But Cassidy liked his machine bathed in diesel oil.

So here I was, in the back of this big machine. It was like a house; I bet it was at least thirty by fifty feet, full of all kinds of gears that were turning. He would turn that machine and stop it and jerk it. Come to think of it, it was really a dangerous position with all those moving parts. It was very loud, and I had no ear protection. It was dark in the back. Before I could get that mop dipped in diesel fuel, I backed into a fan. The mop was still in my back pocket and I lost my balance. The fuzzy mop caught and hit that fan. It blew into a million pieces and was blowing up into the air. Those pieces stuck to everything. It was just like on the movies where someone hits a feather pillow and it blows and sticks to something. When Cassidy saw that, his whole forehead, I promise you, turned red. But because I was the boss's son, all he could do was cuss and holler at me and tell me to clean up every speck of it. So, I did.

He wanted me there an hour before the machine cranked up so that we could grease the tracks. Then he wanted me there an hour after the machine shut down. We would normally go from 7 a.m. to 5 p.m. but he wanted me there from 6 a.m. to 6 p.m. That's twelve hours. At that time, the rock quarry really needed the rock. They could sell all the rock they could produce. So, the rock quarry was running 24/7. Cassidy's shift was seven days a week, so my hours were forty hours regular and forty hours overtime. I was making $2.25 an hour, and when you figure that up, back in those days in 1965, that was a lot of money for a young man. But my dad made me put it in the bank; I couldn't touch it.

Cassidy was so grouchy. He would make me walk to the repair shop where we kept the oil and where broken-down machinery was repaired. He had an old beat-up pickup truck that I could have driven over a dirt road straight to the shop a quarter mile away, but he made me walk. Then I would have to carry back two cans of real heavy grease. So, I would walk maybe a hundred yards and set them down, walk a hundred yards and set them down. But I didn't complain. I was determined to work very hard and to do the best job that I could. So, it was always, "Yes sir, Mr. Cassidy." It would make him mad because he couldn't make me mad. I would continually work harder than anybody ever had, and so from that I gained his favor.

Before too long he was showing me how to run that machine. He had never shown another oiler how to run the machine. I know it was because of the favor of my dad to a measure.

I tell you this story because I'm trying to speak to you, my heritage, and whoever else will listen. I believe in work. I started out at my first job working eighty hours a week, seven days a week. Somehow it seems like the American young people have gotten away from a good work ethic. I didn't have my boys work quite like that, but they work very hard at what they do. Johnathan is a doctor and Isaac is a lawyer. They both are great at what they do. I am so very proud of them.

I also believe that I'm teaching you that if you will work as hard as you can, be diligent, don't complain, and use "Yes, sir" and

"No, sir," you will rise up the ladder. Before it was over, I was running that machine.

And so, my heritage, I say do it this way…

"Whatever you do, work at it with all your heart, as working for the Lord, not for human masters, since you know that you will receive an inheritance from the Lord as a reward. It is the Lord Christ you are serving." Colossians 3:23-24 NIV

Chapter Six

That's The Man

This story has to do with the beginning of the relationship of Debra Marie Pigott and John Isaac Newlin. We met in 1967 in the cafeteria at Fort Myers High School during lunch. Debbie was 15 and I was 16. She was a freshman and I was a sophomore.

I noticed this cute little brunette sitting with some girls across from me on the other side of the long cafeteria table. I was sitting on the opposite side of the table with some boys. I thought, "She's so cute, she has such a cute smile." She looked at me and then looked down. Something about her shyness and her smile made me think she was attracted to me. I knew I was attracted to her.

Yes, I was attracted to her and have been ever since. When I look at her today, I see her beauty, the same as that first day! It doesn't matter if it's early morning when we first get up, mid-day or late at night.
She later confided to me that during that first meeting when we looked into each other's eyes across that cafeteria table, the Lord spoke to her in a loud voice and said, "That's the man

you're going to marry." I thank the Lord that He did that. Spoke to her? What a concept; that you could hear the Lord. She has always had a faith that inspires me. Her faith is profoundly simple and simply profound.

That next Friday night I went to the Bee Hive. It was a place where high school kids went to dance. A band named The Bees played at The Bee Hive. Well, I went to the dance and I saw Debbie and my heart did a flip. I got up enough nerve to ask her to dance. I especially liked the slow dance and she later said she loved my maroon mohair sweater. I took her home and kissed her good night on the front steps. She was 15 and I was 16. It felt like the car floated back home. Our first date was to the fair. I'll never forget her white tight jeans. She had such a cute perfect figure. We have had a date to the fair every year since for 45 years.

She is my God girl. She knew it ever since she heard "That's the man..."

Debbie is gold!

"The man who finds a wife finds a treasure, and he receives favor from the LORD." Proverbs 18:22 NLT

I love her more than ever!

Chapter Seven

Have Your Cake and Eat It Too

When I was a boy, my dad was so good to me. He provided a boat I could fish in. He would pay for the storage and the gas. Many times, I would go fishing by myself. I love to be with people, but many times I've gone fishing and hunting and camping and spent the weekend by myself.

When I was fourteen, my dad would let me use the boat by myself. It would fly across the water and with no windshield, the wind in your face was glorious. I love that feeling you get looking at the fast approaching water with the sun sparkling on it.

I had a trash can on board that would hold probably 30 gallons of water. I put the electric aerator into the trash can and plugged it to the battery, and the aerator would cause air bubbles to be in the trash can so that I could keep bait alive. The trash can aerator is a key ingredient in baking this cake. One evening I decided I was going to go catch a snook on Long Bar. Long Bar is a quarter mile long oyster shell bar on the north side of the Caloosahatchee River. To me, snook are the greatest game fish.

My mother dropped me off at the marina because I wasn't old enough to drive. I took the boat and I went to Long Bar. I fished hard, but I couldn't catch a fish. I finally caught a five-pound redfish, which was a prized fish to eat. I caught that redfish and walked back over to my boat. I was wading on Long Bar. I put that redfish in that bait well (or bait trash can), and it kept that redfish alive. I went back to fishing for snook and couldn't catch any. I thought, "Well, I wonder if that redfish would make a good bait for a Jewfish."

A Jewfish's more politically correct name is a Goliath grouper, but back in those days we just called it a Jewfish. They would hang out underneath the Sanibel Causeway that went from Punta Rassa across to Sanibel Island.

In the span or section of the causeway where a boat could go under the bridge, they have what is called a fender made from wood, and these pylons that go down into the bottom. The Jewfish would hang around those pylons.

Normally, I would use a fish called Jack Cravelle for bait. What we would do to locate Jacks is look for birds feeding over the jacks striking bait fish. You could see those the birds out in the distance in the Bay, then you run to those birds and cast a plug and you'd catch a jack. We'd keep them alive in the bait well (the trash can with the aerator) and run to the bridge causeway.

We'd put down what we called a Jewfish rig, which consisted of a rope, some quarter inch chain maybe six or eight feet long, and a big hook. That hook was forged out of steel and wouldn't bend, and the hook was almost about the size of your hand, as far as the curve of the hook. It was a big open hook, and you'd hook it up through the jack's lips from underneath the bottom part of his jaw up through the top part of his jaw. Then we would have a weight on there that would weigh three or four pounds, and that would take the jack fish down through the current by these pylons.

The jack fish has an unusual sound it makes called grunting: "grunt, grunt, grunt." As soon as that jack fish would start grunting under the water, the Jewfish would come swimming to it. The Jewfish would range anywhere from 50 to 400 pounds. If we caught one over 100 pounds, we were disappointed because we couldn't eat them, but we could sell them if they were under 100 pounds for a nickel a pound. The biggest Jewfish I ever caught was when my brother-in-law, Butch, and I were fishing in the mouth of the Caloosahatchee River (the Sanibel Causeway is out a little past the mouth of this river). There was a larger marker with a set of five pylons, the first one up-river from Punta Rassa. My brother-in-law, Butch, got me into Jewfish fishing and snook fishing.

When I was a boy of about ten, we put down a dead mullet on a Jewfish rig, Butch got a good hit and set the hook and he and I could barely pull it up. I was amazed at the size of it. It looked like it could be seven or eight feet long and three or four feet wide. We finally got up to the boat, cut a hole in its lip, tied a rope to it and tied it to the cleat on the back of the boat. It was too big to lift in the boat, so, we slowly motored it to Punta Rassa. It took six men to pull it up on the dock and it weighed 450 pounds. That was the biggest one I have ever seen live. The record Jewfish is over 600 pounds. They are a protected species now.

Well, on this day I was fishing for Jewfish, and I was using a redfish for bait. I had never used a five-pound redfish for bait. Yes, the one I caught on long bar. I was by myself, so I tied up to the fender, under the causeway, the one closest to Punta Rassa. I got up on top of the fender where there's a walkway. I walked down and dropped that redfish down alive in my favorite spot. It needed to be an incoming tide, and it was. Right off the bat—BAM!—I got a hit and I hooked onto a good old Jewfish. I pulled and tugged and got him up to the surface. I saw he wasn't extremely big, and I was glad because I was hoping to eat him. They weren't too good to eat over 100 pounds.

I pulled him over and around the end of the pylon and brought him over to the boat. I eased down onto the boat and got down to the back of the boat. I reached down and cut a hole in his bottom lip, put a rope through it, tied him off, tied him to the cleat, and I had him. He was mine.

I took a little rest, then thought, "Well, I need to pull him up into the boat." I untied him from the cleat and tried to pull him in the boat, but I couldn't get him up over the side of the boat. I was just a young boy, about fourteen, and I couldn't get him over the side. I could get his head up just to the edge of what we called the gunnel, or the gunwale, but I couldn't get him over the side. Then I got up on the side of the gunnel and tried to pick him up and I couldn't do it. So, I put him back down in the water and walked to the back and tied him to a cleat.

I sat down on a cooler, took a rest and tried to think of a solution. There were no boats in sight, and I was too proud to ask for help anyway. Then I thought, "What if I had a handle?" I went up under the front of the boat where I had a ski rope with a wooden handle. It had a wooden handle and the rope was tied to each end, then it came together to a single rope that a person would use to ski. I took that back there, and right where it joined together into a single rope, I tied it through his lip. Then I went over to the side of the boat and I climbed up on the side. I was standing on the side of the boat about three feet above the bottom of the boat.

Now I had a handle. I got him up and almost got his head over. Finally, his head came over. My feet slipped out from under me and I fell three feet flat on my back! Then that big Jewfish came right down and landed on my chest. Now they've got spines on their backs that are as big around as your finger, and they're real sharp. If that spine of a dorsal fin would've landed in that position on me, it would have stuck me in the chest and probably killed me. As it was, it totally knocked the breath out of me. First, my back hit the floor, and second, that fish hit my chest. I was knocked out of breath and couldn't breathe, and I was gasping for air, but I was really trying to figure out if anybody saw what happened because I was so embarrassed. I finally peeked my head over the side of the boat, looked up, and there wasn't anybody around. It took me, what seemed like ten minutes, before I could even get a breath. But I was proud. And guess what? I forgot to tell you, but guess what was in the mouth of that Jewfish? My redfish! So, I got my redfish out of its mouth and I was going to have supper with him, and then I had that big old Jewfish. It was like having my cake and eating it too.

It seems in life, sometimes things do work out. Sometimes you need to take a risk. Risk what you have for something better. It may take work and a little boldness; it may take your breath away but go for it, my heritage. Especially, in the spiritual, like Elisha in the Bible, go for the double portion. Sometimes you can have your cake and eat it too.

God knows I love to fish!

Chapter Eight

Stripped and Hand-lined

When I was a boy of sixteen, my dad was so good to me. He had a boat that was a 20-foot Lyndcraft with a 100 horsepower Evinrude outboard motor. My dad was so generous, he let me use that boat anytime I wanted, and he paid for the gas.

He kept the boat in a dry storage marina on the Caloosahatchee River. I fished quite a bit, sometimes day and night. My favorite fish was called a snook. A snook is famous with the people that do fish for it. Many people don't know about snook, but to me it's the greatest fish there is as far as sport fishing.

I took that 20-foot Lyndcraft and removed the seats and the windshield off it. I put two coolers down for seats. With these changes it was open and much more fishable. It was mainly just a fishing boat.

Oh, the passion for catching snook. A snook, for some people, is very hard to catch. For other people, if you knew how to catch them, it was easy. They feed on certain tides, certain baits, and certain holes. I loved to fish for them with top water plugs, because when they would hit and strike the plug, it was such a good heart rush.

One of my favorite places to fish for snook was called Long Bar. It was an oyster bar at the mouth of the Caloosahatchee River near Fort Myers, Florida. It was longer than most oyster bars; it ran for almost a quarter of a mile. Some snook fishermen knew about it, but most didn't. Even when I was a boy, in the summertime, nobody would be fishing on Long Bar.

What I liked to do was pull up to the bar in my boat, anchor it and get out. We'd have to wear tennis shoes to keep our feet from getting cut up on the oysters. We would wade and fish. We would work from one end of the bar on the outside, then we'd go all the way around and we'd work the inside of the bar. What made that bar so good was a deep cut up next to some mangrove trees on the inside of the bar. That trough ran almost to the mangroves at one end.

On certain days we would really get into the snook on that bar. We would use a spinning rod or a casting rod with a 20-pound test line. We started out using Zara Spooks, which is a big lure you can throw a long way. Then we switched over to using a greenback floater, Mirror lures, and sometimes a little blue Boone plug.

We would wade that bar, and sometimes the snook would hit your plug right in front of you, and if it was a 20-pound snook it made a large strike on top and it would just stop your heart. Ordinarily a snook is a hard-fighting fish, usually it fights on top of the water. It'll jump and thrash its' head on top, but they don't usually run very far.

The story I'm telling today is one of the most unusual snook fights I ever had or have ever heard. On this day I was fishing with my friend, Bill. I got on a big snook, and the snook ran toward the mangroves. The inside of the bar at the south end isn't too far from the mangroves, but it isn't that close either. It is about 100 yards. On the outside of the bar was the Caloosahatchee River, which was almost a mile wide.

So, I was fishing inside the bar and I got this big snook on, and he jumped one time and shook his head. He was huge—he looked like he might have been somewhere between 25 and 30 pounds, which would be the biggest snook I ever caught. We just hollered with joy when we saw how big he was. This snook, though, began to run and I couldn't stop him. I had a 20-pound test line on an Ambassador casting reel; I didn't have that much line. But normally with 20-pound test line you could hold back on a snook and he wouldn't break it unless you had to just stop him right there.

So, he began ripping line off that reel. God knows I love that sound. I had my thumb on the spool to increase the drag. My pole was bent just about flat towards the mangroves. I was over waist deep and could not follow that big snook because of the deep cut in front of me. I saw I was starting to get low on my line. I never, ever had a snook strip all my line. Stripping means you'd run out of line, and the line would go out through the pole and you'd lose the line and whatever was on the end of it.

I put pressure on it, and I thought I was going to break the 20-pound test line. I waded in until I was chest deep, almost to my neck. He was taking it right to the mangroves. He jumped one time close to the mangroves and I thought, "Oh my God, he's gonna wrap me in the mangroves." At about that time he turned and started heading towards the bar. I was rejoicing because I was able to get more than a few cranks back on my line. Now, it looked like he was going to go out across the bar towards the river.

So, I had to hold my pole way up high, as high as I could. My arms were straight up, with the pole straight up. I held tension on the line so that when he crossed that bar, the line wouldn't hit the oysters and get cut. Well, here he goes across the bar. He's going out toward the river and I can't stop him. It was the same thing; my line was rip, rip, rip, my drag's going out, out, out. So, I started wading out. It was a little shallower and flatter going out at a gradual rate towards the river from the bar. I followed him, and it was like he was pulling me. I finally got out to neck deep and could not go any deeper without my head going under. He was either going to break me off or strip me. At about that time he turned again.

Now, some people may be reading this and if they're a snook fisherman, they're going to say, "Uh huh, I caught this guy now. He is a liar, because a snook does not fight that long and does not pull out that much line." I would have called myself a liar because I've caught many snook since then, and never have I come close to having one strip me, much less twice now in one fight: the first time in towards the mangroves, the second time out towards the river.

I finally turned him, and here he goes, heading back toward the bar again. So, I was rejoicing again; I thought I'd got this snook worn out. I'm back in line! I got up on the bar and I held my pole way up over my head again with my arms as high as I could. Here he goes back across the bar and I've got enough tension, and he doesn't cut me off on oysters. He goes across, and I'm fighting him. He shakes his head again, and now he's headed for the mangroves again. Once again, I cannot believe it. Here he is—strip, strip, strip, strip, taking line off my reel. By this time Billy was right with me. Forget him fishing; we had a huge snook on.

All of a sudden, here he goes again ripping line; now, I'm not so excited about the sound--strip, strip, strip. Suddenly, he strips it all out. There goes my line, out through the end of the pole, and I've lost him. I couldn't believe it. I'm standing there with an empty reel, an empty pole. It was the biggest snook I've ever had in my life and he stripped me. There I was, standing there stripped. I took my pole and I threw it down into the water. I was just so mad. Old Billy, he comes over, picks my pole up out of the water and says, "Come on John, that was great. Don't get that mad." So, I got to thinking about it and I thought, "Yeah, that was great."

I went back over to my boat, which was parked on the outside of the bar, and I got another pole out of the boat. This time it was a spinner rod. I had on a pair of shorts and sneakers, with no shirt; we were wade fishing there. I started fishing again. I was walking along, and all of a sudden, I felt some line on my leg. I said, "Billy! I feel a line; I think it's my line!" So, I grabbed it by hand. That's why I say, "Stripped and Hand lined." I've got the line in my hand and I start pulling, and I have that snook on. He shakes his head and he's over underneath the mangroves. Now he's further south, down by where the mangroves are closer to the end of Long Bar.

So now I've got him on by hand, and guess what he does? He jumps up, and he gets the hook of the Mirror lure caught on a branch. Now there's my snook, hanging by a branch his head out of the water. He was worn out and about half dead. So, I'm thinking, "Well, I'm going to swim across the channel between the bar and the mangroves." But it's pretty deep there, so I back up onto the bar and I run the best I can on those sharp oysters down to where the bar gets closer to the mangroves.

Billy and I start wading across, and guess what we see? A bull shark. The bull shark has got his fin out of the water about eight inches, which means he's a very big bull shark. I don't know what you know about sharks, but bull sharks are some of the worst ones that I fear, even more than hammerheads, maybe more than a tiger. A bull shark, if he wants to mess with you, he'll mess with you until he hurts you. I've caught lots of sharks and read lots of shark stories. So, here's a bull shark, ten feet away from me, coming directly at me. The water is not clear, he's coming ten feet from me, and all I've got is a net in my hand to protect me.

Billy said, "John, what do we do?"

I said, "Stand still!"

At about that time, the bull shark disappeared, without a swirl, without anything, he disappears. There's the snook over there, hanging in the mangrove tree, and I can't move because I'm afraid to move.

I said, "I've got to move, Billy."

I start slowly wading towards my snook, and before I could get my net under him, he shook his head one more time and he dropped off, and my Mirror lure was hanging in the tree. The big snook slipped beneath the dark brackish water and was swept away like a dream, like the memory swept away by the current of time. I got my lure back to confirm the memory of the big snook that Stripped and Hand-lined me.

Chapter Nine

Root Picker on #63 Shaker

This story finds me working at the rock quarry. Each summer when school was out, I went back to work at the quarry. I'd have to find a new job because somebody else would be in the position I was in the summer before, so I had to do whatever job was open.

The job in this story was called a root picker. I worked over a large conveyor belt about four feet across, made of thick, heavy rubberized material. This conveyor belt started right underneath the main rock crusher. Rocks would come in from the portable crusher, go up the big belt and go into the main crusher. The crusher was called a hammer mill.

It's hard to describe exactly what a hammer mill is. The actual hammers are large pieces of extremely hard steel that would rotate over and over, and when the hammer would hit the rocks it would crush them. The crushed rock would fall on the fast-moving conveyor belt. My job was to pick out any trash (usually roots) out of the crushed rock.

Many times, when the drag line would be digging up the rock from underneath the water, it would have these big tree roots in it. They would go through the portable crusher also, and then they would go through the crusher. But they wouldn't go to pieces; a lot of times they would still be stuck in a mashed-up root that would be heavy, and the smell was horrible.

My new job was to sit at the bottom of that crusher where the belt came out, and when I saw a big root, I was to grab it and pull it off the belt. Sometimes it would be too big, and I'd have to turn loose of it.

There were several things about this job that were unique. One was that it was a ten hour a day job. Another was that it was so loud. In those days we didn't have ear protection. We should have, but we just didn't. I don't think there was any OSHA requirement about it. I would sit there, on a cut-off 55-gallon drum. The first day I didn't even have a cushion to put on the rim, so after about thirty seconds my butt hurt. After about half an hour I thought I was about to die. I finally got a two by four to put across there. The next day I brought a boat cushion.

Getting back to how loud it was, it was so loud—you won't believe this—but I took a pipe in my hand and hit a piece of pipe in front of me, and I couldn't even hear one pipe strike the other pipe. That is extremely loud. The extreme noise of that crusher was going on ten hours a day, right next to me. But not just that—there was continual dripping of muddy water —I thought it was like Chinese water torture. I had on a hard hat and the water would drip and hit my hard hat, and sometimes go down the back of my shirt.

Then these rocks would come flying from out of the top

44

of that crusher. Occasionally, a rock would hit me in the head (thank God I had the hard hat on), or one would hit me in the shoulder bone, and it would make me so mad I wanted to cry.

There was also a vibration that was very strong as you were sitting there. And there was the smell of those roots. I'm telling you, after about one minute, it seemed like an eternity for a boy. To have to be there ten hours a day—it was unbelievable.

That's where my dad had me. It was a very dangerous job. When the belt would stop, it meant something was broken down, and everybody would have to jump up to go find out what was wrong and help. But I was so tired that when that belt stopped one day, I just put my head down on this metal rail made of pipe that was in front of me and I went to sleep. I felt a rock hit me right in the chest. I looked up, and there was my old man standing there staring at me. He threw the rock that hit me. He just said, "You need to come down." He never got on my case about that time when I was sleeping on the job, He never mentioned it again but he's the one that hit me with that rock! Haha!!

Another amazing thing was you could sit there, and that belt was steady rolling, kind of going from low on the right to going way up on the left. It seemed like it was going by ninety-to-nothing; I don't know how fast it was going, but it was traveling very fast. You got so used to that belt going in one direction that whenever they would stop it, it was a strange phenomenon that would happen in your head. In your head, when the belt stopped, the belt looked like it started going backwards. It looked like it was running the other way, just steady running. You had to put your hand out to prove to yourself that the belt had stopped. As soon as you took your hand away and just looked at it for a second, it would take off going backwards again. It wasn't moving backwards; it was all in your head.

So, when I hear somebody complain about their job, about how hard it is, I think in my mind, "They should have worked as a... "Root Picker on the #63 Shaker."

I thank God for that experience.

"In everything give thanks, for this is the will of God in Christ Jesus concerning you." I Thess. 5:18 KJV

This verse is one of my life verses. It is a secret to contentment.

Chapter Ten

Pig Tied

This story starts when we were going to rope a bull. It's like another story called "You Got a Locomotive Now," where I tell about roping a bull. In this story, we were in a different pasture that was thick. It had grown thick with trees called myrtle trees, which is actually a great wood to cook steaks over.

We had a herd of wild Brahma cows in this pasture that had to be moved to another pasture across the county. When we went to work the cows, our big mean Brahma bull jumped our outside fence.

My old man said, "We'll get that bull when the other landowners work their cows."
We worked the cows and hauled them away. There were about 200 head of cows and calves. The next day when we drove back past that pasture, sure enough that bull was back in that pasture again by himself. We decided we needed to rope him. Big Man had a twinkle in his eye and a grin on his face. I suspect I did too.

This time it was a different cowboy crew. This time

there were five guys on horseback: my dad, myself, Jack, Wayne, and Big Man. Jack was about my dad's age. They were both in their sixties, and to be on horseback in your sixties is kind of unusual. Wayne was my age. Then we had my best friend Big Man Flint, who I was always in competition with. He could out-fight me, out-rope me, and out-ride me. It seemed I would take a chance on dying just to beat him.

We all started off riding side by side, then, we went in different directions, looking for this bull. As I said, it was a pasture, but it had so many small trees growing up that you could hardly see for any distance in one direction. I took a direction and after about twenty minutes, I came around a corner, and there was the bull, standing there with his back to some myrtles.

There's a cardinal rule among cowboys that you never, ever rope a bull by yourself. If you do, you don't have much control over that bull. He can pull your saddle off your horse, or he can get you wrapped up with your horse and you and your horse can get hurt or killed.

Like I said, he was backed up against a thicket pawing the ground making it fly in the air up over his back. He began blowing and snorting rather loudly. I thought, "Oh no, he is making so much noise the others are going hear him and come over."

You see, as soon as I saw him, I hatched a plan I didn't really want dwell on because I didn't want to talk myself out of it. Right in front of this bull was another myrtle bush, and I had a thought. If I could throw the rope around that bull's neck and get him tight, and then get a wrap on that myrtle in front, I'd have him pulling against the tree. I always kept a small rope about eight feet long on my saddle. We called it our rope to "pig tie" something, to tie up the legs. In fact, in competition rodeo, they'll do calf roping and then pig tie the calf that they've roped.

I couldn't help myself. I threw my loose lay, which is my regular roping rope, around that bull's neck and it came up tight. It happened just like I wanted it to. I got a wraparound that myrtle, jumped off my horse, Fred, undid the roping rope from the saddle horn and tied it to that myrtle. Now that bull was pulling back as hard as he could against that rope. He began to get a little bit choked, so he didn't pay much attention to me down on the ground. I was able to throw my pig tie rope between his legs and just missed getting kicked. I took a stick and pulled the small rope to where I could reach it. Sure enough, I pulled it up tight and he fell down and I pig tied him. I tied his two hind legs to his front legs, and I undid the rope around his neck. There he was, laying there. I gathered my rope up and got up on my horse, Fred, then started looking for the other guys. I was feeling really good, but I didn't want it to show.

In the meantime, they had come back together. The pasture wasn't that big. Here they came, riding up, and Jack said, "Anybody seen him?"
What was unusual about this fellow named Jack was that he had the deepest voice of any man I think I've ever heard. Sometimes I think he tried to make it deep. He said it again, "Anybody seen him?" in a deep voice.

I said, "I've got him tied up right over here."

In his deepest voice, Old Big Man—I think he was trying to imitate Jack—he said, "Bullshit!"

I said, "No Big Boy, I've got him tied up right over here."

I think I heard him say, "Yeah, we'll see."

So we rode over. When they saw that big old bull, pig tied, laying there, Big Man just couldn't believe it. We rode around to get the horse trailer to load him up.

It was one of the few times that my old man ever paid me a good compliment. I called him Dad, but the grandkids called him Papa Newlin. He was so tight; he never would give much of a compliment. But when we were riding back, me just a little taller in the saddle, we were side by side, and he didn't want the other guys to hear him. He said, "Good job, son." It felt really good. I took that as a real compliment, especially coming from him.

That round went to the Newlins. In my mind that day and even now, in my memory, the Big Bull and the Big Man got...Pig Tied.

Chapter Eleven

Big Man's Rodeo

This is another story about Big Man. As I described Big Man earlier, he was just something else to me. He was a young man, he was just nineteen, but he acted thirty.

He could out rope and outride and outfight me. We had a tremendous competition in everything we did. It didn't matter if we were throwing knives at the barn or if we were practicing roping bales of hay at the barn, but especially when we were roping live steers or cows or heifers, calves or big bulls, we were very, very competitive.

Big Man worked for a man named Bass. Everybody called him Bass. He was an old man at that time, and he happened to be a friend of my dad's. Bass had several ranches, and Big Man's dad, Clyde, would look after Bass's cattle and Arabian horses.

Big Man's family lived in a trailer on Mr. Bass's property. Mr. Bass had a section of land that was fenced and didn't have a set of cow pens on it.

One day, they found out that his cattle had pinkeye. When cattle have pinkeye, they need to be treated, and you have to put some medicine in their eyes. When you don't have pens, you've got to catch the cattle, and about the only way to do that is to rope them.

You've never seen anybody so happy in all his life, when Big Man found out that we had to rope all those cattle. You better believe it made me happy, too.

This was a big ranch, wide open prairies where you could really run and chase cattle. One morning Big Man and I had our eye on a big, healthy heifer (you might call her a cow, but a heifer is a cow that hasn't had a calf) that weighed somewhere around 700 pounds, at least. She might have weighed more. She was part Angus and part Brahma and she could really run.

Big Man was riding an Arabian horse and when she would get to running, that tail would be up and flying in the wind like a flag. My horse couldn't run near as fast, even though I rode a purebred quarter horse named Fred.

So, we were chasing this one Brangus heifer, and Big Man had the lead. He threw and MISSED, which was a rarity. Normally, we have two ropes, but before Big Man could get to his second rope, here I was coming on Fred at a dead run. He knew I was going to have a shot at that same heifer, and it would have just been horrible to him if he had missed and I roped it.

So Big Man got to going even faster. Instead of slowing to get his second rope, he rode up next to that heifer and leaned over in the saddle and grabbed her by the tail. Now as he's riding, he's got a hold of the cow's tail, leaned way over. Then, unbelievably, he stepped out of the saddle and into a dead run, and as he's got a hold of that tail, all of a sudden, he's running, she's running, and he gets to slinging that cow around in a circle, by the tail. Three full revolutions! She goes down and Big Man stands on top of her with one foot and says, "Now beat that, John Newlin!" I'm thinking "not a chance, even in my dreams." This round goes to Big Man. There will be other rounds.

But this one was truly... "Big Man's Rodeo."

Chapter Twelve

Big Man's Double Handled Hat And Other Stories of Big Man

This is another story about Big Man. My dad, Big Man and I were on horseback on a prairie on Bass Ranch. We were roping cattle and treating them for pink eye. My dad and I were sitting side by side looking out across the prairie into a beautiful sunset.

We saw Big Man riding at least 500 yards away, perhaps further. He was chasing a steer, trying to rope it, but the steer was going at a dead run. This particular property had ditches in it that would irrigate a crop and every couple hundred yards there would be an old irrigation ditch. Big Man, riding his Arab mare with her trademark tail flying high in the wind, was right on the steer's heels.

The steer would jump an irrigation ditch, followed by that Arab mare with Big Man silhouetted against the orange-yellow sky. The old man and I were entranced in the moment. "It doesn't get any better than this," I thought to myself.

They came to the next ditch and the steer jumped it clear, but when Big Man's horse went to jump the ditch, she stumbled. She rolled, and Big Man flew off the horse, landed on the ground and rolled. My dad and I silently gasped because we thought he might have been hurt badly, maybe killed. But he came up out of that roll and picked up his hat, and with both hands he pulled that hat down on his head hard. Then he got back on his horse.

Just the action of pulling his hat down on his head double handed, made my dad and I laugh so hard we almost fell off our horses. You had to have been there, I guess. We laughed, partly from relief, but I think we laughed identifying with his embarrassment, anger, and wholehearted resolve evident by the way he pulled that hat down on his head.

It was a rare and precious moment laughing with my dad sitting there on horseback. We looked in each other's eyes and knew we had seen a thing. We both knew why we loved Big Man.

Another story about Big Man is when he was chasing another steer through thick woods; this time at another ranch. Once again at full speed trying to rope a steer. The steer made a sharp right, and his horse went straight ahead and stopped suddenly. Big Man flew off into a myrtle tree that was about six feet high. I didn't see him do that but found out later when he told us what happened.

Big Man came up missing. We couldn't find him. We rode and rode, and finally saw his horse standing under a myrtle tree. Big Man was in that myrtle tree, knocked out, spread out like an eagle. He was unconscious. We carefully lowered him down out of that tree and revived him back to life, and he got up and kept right on working.

Another time, Big Man and I were working, stretching fence. We were working a stretch of a quarter mile at a time. We had stretched the wire so incredibly tight we felt the tension in our souls. When we had it stretched, we had to push the barbed wire into the post to be able to nail it. When Big Man pushed it, the barbed wire broke and cut right through the palm of Big Man's hand, deeper than a quarter inch. It was heavily bleeding all the way across the width of his hand. He took his handkerchief off, wrapped it up tight, and never stopped.

Later that evening, we were working cows in a cow pen, having to catch them. There he was, catching those calves by the hind leg. All he had was that dirty hanky thing wrapped around his deeply cut hand and there was cow dung and dirt getting in his hand.

That was Big Man, he never complained, and he never stopped working. That would have been beneath his dignity. He was Big Man. That was a small sign of his big resolve.

I will always love and never forget my friend.

Resolve: "I set my face like flint"

"I gave my back to the smiters, and my cheeks to them that plucked off the hair: I hid not my face from shame and spitting. For the Lord God will help me; therefore, shall I not be confounded: therefore, have I set my face like a flint, and I know that I shall not be ashamed." Isa. 50: 6,7 KJV

Chapter Thirteen

Changes in Attitudes Or Where Da Damn Sack

This story started around the year 1976. I went coon hunting with my favorite neighbor, Wayne, one cool clear night in December. We were both young Georgia farmers at the time, although I was born in West Virginia and raised in Florida. We hunted on our farms and on neighboring farms.

On this night, we had two special guests with us. They were two young black men from an unnamed place in the country, about twenty miles north of our farm that was seven miles north of Whigham, Georgia. They were brothers, and their names were Willie Mac and Marvin.

Willie Mac was older and smaller, but industrious and ambitious, and definitely the brains of their outfit. He had a reputation for being a good coon hunter, and we were glad he had brought a couple of good-looking dogs. One was a Bluetick and the other a Plot. I had never hunted with those types of dogs before, or those types of men. Things were really looking interesting to me.

Marvin had a marvelous physique. He was all of 6'4",

with broad shoulders and a narrow waist. He carried effortlessly a huge double-bladed axe. Being an axe man, in my own mind, I was intrigued by the size and weight of that axe head. I probably used a five-pound axe head and I thought it was big; this axe weighed ten pounds if it weighed an ounce. At first, I kept a close eye on him and that big axe, but soon I heard the gentleness of his heart in his voice and saw it in his eyes, and I relaxed, knowing he was on my side.

Wayne was about 5'8", sort of thin framed, with red hair. But he was a wiry man, and at times he would be a little bit angry. That night he seemed to be a little bit angry; he was grouchy. He would walk ahead of us and we would follow him. Because he was grouchy, I think we all got a little bit grouchy. We hunted from a little after dark until almost midnight and hadn't even had our dogs strike a good trail.

As was my custom, I would carry a little flask of whiskey. This was back in the days when I wasn't walking too closely with the Lord. I'd take a shot of that whiskey every once in a while, when they weren't looking. Wayne went to church, and Willie Mac went to church. I didn't much want to talk to them about me having a shot, but it kind of eased my attitude a bit when everybody was so grouchy.

This night, we weren't doing any good catching coons, and I said I needed to take a little break and go to the bathroom. I slipped off, found a stump, and had myself a shot of that whiskey. About that time one of those coon hounds came over and started barking.

I thought, "You dumb dog, you're barking at me."

Then I heard the guys coming, so I had to put my flask up. Sure enough, that dog was tree barking, and it was right by the tree I was near. So, we started shining our lights up the tree. It was a very tall tree, at least 100 feet, and I don't really know the species or the name of it.

Somebody said, "Wow! Look at that coon! He is a BIG coon!"

It was a big fat boar coon (a boar coon is a male coon). As was our custom, we would generally shoot them out with a .22 and let the dogs fight them. But sometimes I would climb the tree and shake out the coon. Willie Mac wanted to catch a live coon to train his puppies with, so I said, "I'll climb up there and shake him out."

I had a saying that God never made a tree that I couldn't climb. That was pretty proud and cocky, and not true, of course, but that was my saying. So, I started climbing, and the coon started going higher, so I started going higher, too.

I had a stout leather belt that was pretty soft. When I came to a tree that didn't have any lower limbs, I would throw it around the tree and if I could get my other hand on that belt, then I would stretch my legs up (if I had on jeans) and scooch up a little bit. This one was too big to wrap my legs around, but I would slide the belt up a bit, scooch up again, slide the belt up until I could get to a limb. That was really tough work.

By the time I got to that first limb, I was already shaking and a little bit tired. In those days I was still an athlete and in my own mind, just about an acrobat. I wasn't afraid to climb anything.

So, I got up to a limb to climb higher and higher, and finally got up close to that big coon. I didn't realize how big he was. He was a big boar coon that looked like he weighed somewhere between 15 and 20 pounds. When he saw me, he started showing his teeth and growling.

I thought, "Oh great, I need a long stick."

I climbed back down a little to where I could get the

right size limb, and I took my knife and cut a stick about six feet long. It might have been an inch through; it was a pretty stout stick. I got up there and started trying to poke the coon, but he wanted to fight and bite rather than jump. He was trying to get to me! All of a sudden, I had a coon on my hands, and I was sword-fighting with that coon. Finally, I got him just right and I pushed him out. I saw him sailing down. It seemed like it took forever for him to hit the ground. As I looked down, there was a ruckus down there. I could see these little tiny flashlights way down at the bottom of the tree.

I was just watching, enjoying it, and all of a sudden, I thought, "I'm missing out on all the fun, I've gotta get down there!"

So I started to climb down, maybe a bit hastily, and I slipped. I fell for about three feet with my hands on either side of that tree. The bark on that tree was an unusual bark; I don't remember seeing many trees just like it. It was a rough bark, with little checkerboard squares on it with gaps in between. When my hands scraped along on that bark, it tore the hide right off the inside of my hands. It cut them a quarter inch deep. I thank God that somehow, I've got a mechanism in me that I call my shock factor. I think it was a rush of adrenaline; I didn't really feel pain in my hands. Thank God I caught myself and didn't fall all the way down; I would have been dead for sure.

My hands felt a little bit like they were on fire, but they didn't really hurt like extreme pain. They were burning. So, I just made up my mind to ignore it and climbed on down. When I got down there was an incredible ruckus or a good fight in coon hunting terms.

Coon dogs will try to fight and catch and kill the coon. But coon dogs are really a lot more bark than they are bite. They don't really know how to kill a coon quickly. They'll grab him and shake him some, but about the time they get scratched or bit they turn loose.

If I had my cow dogs, which were sometimes used as hog dogs, a coon wouldn't have a chance. In a matter of probably ten seconds, he's dead. They just put their whole mouth over his skull and crunch. They don't try to play, they don't bark, they just kill a coon. But these dogs weren't like that. They were fighting this coon, and he was so big that he would get on his back, and he was fighting them and fussing. The dogs were barking like crazy, the men were shouting, and the big coon was hissing and growling. It was wonderful pandemonium!

Willie Mac had a croaker sack with him, and he sat the sack down. Next thing you know, Willie Mac had that coon by the tail, and he started hollering, "Where Da Sack? Where Da Damn Sack?!"

I think I was the next in line with nerve, and I grabbed the sack and tried to open it up and get the coon in it. Between the dogs trying to grab the coon and us trying to keep the dogs away from the coon, and Willie Mac holding the coon by the tail (if you get a hold of a coon by the tail he can't really turn on you, as long as he doesn't grab your pants leg or your shirt)....this coon was big. The sack was actually a burlap bag, a feed sack. When I tried to hold that sack open, the coon caught the side of the sack with his hand. Then he reached and got my hand and made a terrible screaming growling sound as he tried to bite my hand. I had no choice but to turn loose of that sack. About that time Willie Mac turned loose of the coon.

Now we had a big giant coon/dog fight, and we were all hollering and going around and around the tree. The noise level was cranked up another notch! Next news you know, I saw a coon tail, and somehow, I grabbed the coon tail. Guess what I said?

I said, "Where Da Sack? Where Da Damn Sack?"

I said it just like that black man. "Da sack"? I think you emulate sometimes in the midst of something like that. I think I sounded just like him. So, Willie Mac, now being the next in line for bravery, grabbed the sack. When he held that sack open and I lifted the coon up, that coon grabbed the side of the sack. Again!! He reached and grabbed Willie Mac's hand and tried to bite him and did scratch him. But Willie Mac didn't turn loose of the sack and I got him in the sack. We grabbed the top of that sack, and you have never heard such whooping like Indians (although we were black and white Indians). We were hollering and dancing and shouting. We had a "Change In Attitude!"

What happened next is Willie Mac said, "Look what that coon did to my hand!"

We looked, and he had a pretty deep scratch on that hand.

I said, "Yeah, look what he did to mine!"

I turned mine over, and they were a bloody mess. I hadn't seen it up until then in all the excitement; I hadn't really looked at them. They all went, "Oh my God!"

I was silent for a moment.

Then, I said, "No boys, I did that when I fell down that tree."

I'm not sure where God is in this story. I think it just proves I'm rather ordinary and love dogs and adventure. I have found in my latter days that being thankful to God is the best remedy for a poor attitude. Sometimes circumstances can change your attitude.

It did on this night. We were grouchy and then we laughed and shouted. We had the coon in "Da" sack and we really had a "Change in Attitude."

Chapter Fourteen

Dog Gone Irony The Story of Waylon

I've always loved dogs. This is a dog story. I've got quite a few of those that you'll never get to hear, but this one is about a dog named Waylon.

I guess he was named after Waylon Jennings, a famous country singer. Waylon was a coon dog. He was a Black and Tan, which is an actual breed of coon dog. Waylon might not have been a purebred Black and Tan because he wasn't big-boned. When he was a puppy, he had long ears that would drag on the ground. It was so comical you had to chuckle. By the time he was full grown, each ear must have been ten inches long. He was longer in the trunk than most dogs, and a little bit skinny. That and the way he got around just endeared him to the family and anybody that noticed.

I was given Waylon when he was a little puppy. I got him from my neighbor that I would coon hunt with. When we would go coon hunting, I would carry Waylon because he was just too little to follow us and keep up. Pretty soon he was able to follow right behind me. One night, Waylon really got broken into coon hunting right; I guess a dog should if he's going to be a really good coon dog.

This night I was hunting with Wayne, Willie Mack, and his brother Marvin. On this night we got into a terrific run. That means the dogs were hot on the trail of a coon, running fast and hollering, howling-type barking. They soon treed a couple coons up a tall hollow dead tree. The old tree was maybe 50' tall and 3' across the trunk. Marvin always carried this big axe when we went hunting, so he grabbed it and said, "I'll cut it down. It's hollow!"

Wayne said, "Yeah, that tree is no good for timber. It'd be alright—cut it down, Marvin."

I'll tell you what--it was a dangerous thing when big Marvin swung that ten-pound axe. He axed that tree so hard that the chunks would fly off, landing over twenty feet away. The chunks were dangerous, so big that if they hit you, they'd knock you out or cut you. So, we had to stand back when Marvin was chopping. A tree that would take me hours to cut down wouldn't take Marvin but twenty minutes.

Next news you know, we're saying "Timberrrrrr!" and we're pushing over this hollow tree that's got two coons in it. The dogs were going crazy barking. We had three or four good dogs and I had a little puppy there in my arms named Waylon. Those coons would run inside the hollow tree from one end to the other, and the dogs would be there so the coons couldn't get out. There were a couple holes in the side of the tree, and I put Waylon down and he would stick his nose in one of those holes. He was getting himself a snout full of coon scent that night. That's why I say it was so good for him, because he just really got as excited as those other dogs got so excited about those coons.

Well, it warmed up. Seasons change. Life to me is one

transition. Where does time go? Sometimes I'll say, "I haven't seen you in a coon's age". I'm not sure how long the life of a coon is. I do know every coon dies. Every dog dies. In fact, every hundred years all new people. What happens when you die? I love that question. I know the answer. Well that's another story. Let's get back to Waylon's trail.

We only hunted coons in the wintertime. One winter we got 53 coons. I never knew how well other coon hunters did, but I always figured 53 coons in one season was pretty outstanding.

I let my dogs run free on the farm. We lived on a farm in Georgia. It was beautiful; it had so many pecan trees. I just loved the farm. I loved to run that tractor. I would go from can —to—can't from before daylight to dark thirty. I loved to farm.

I had lots of dogs during that time on the farm. I had a dog named Man. I could tell you lots of stories about a dog named Man. He was part bulldog and part Redbone. Well, Man would follow me everywhere I went. No matter where I was on the farm working, I could look up and there would be Man over in the shade, watching me.

Man would follow me, but Waylon would go off in the woods and hunt. Waylon had a different beat to a different drummer. Waylon was obsessed with following his own path now. The trail of the coon.

One summer day I had stopped the tractor and I heard that growing puppy, Waylon, over in the woods barking. It was what we called a tree bark. There's a difference between when a dog is running a coon or even searching for a coon. Even if we had a half a dozen dogs with us, we would know just which dog was "talking" by how they sounded. When they got to a tree bark, it was different. It was repetitive and closer together.

Instead of a howl, it was more of a "bark bark bark bark," just a steady bark. A hot tree bark meant the dog had a coon treed.

When I stopped the tractor, I heard Waylon doing a steady bark. By this time, he was probably about five or six months old. I went to him and lo and behold, there was a coon up in a small tree. Waylon could see him, and he was just sitting at that tree barking at that coon. I thought, "Oh boy, I've got me a coon dog." I couldn't wait for winter.

That next season I started him out hunting with a different group of guys. They were black guys that I played baseball with. In fact, the second season my brother, Jerry, and I were the only white guys in their black baseball league. It was so back in the country the places we played were called names like Coon Bottom or Dry Springs. The home run fences were rows of corn like in the movie "Field of Dreams."

Anyway, I had gotten to know their family very well. There were about a dozen families making one big family clan. The oldest of the family was named Tommy, and I'm really not sure I even know Tommy's last name now. They all called him Tommy; they didn't call him Grandpa Tommy, just Tommy.

I got to know him by trading lighter wood (that's a type of wood that gets really hot when it burns, and it is hard to find). They just loved to cook with it. They would cook their cane syrup over it. They grew sugar cane, and then they would take their mule around the circle mill to press it. They had a big vat that they kept a fire underneath to cook the cane syrup, and they would burn the lighter wood to cook it.

One day they came to me and said, "Hey John, I see you've got lighter wood. Could we buy some?" I said, "Buy some? Come on, we'll give you a truckload of lighter wood."

They made me take some cans of cane syrup in trade. It tastes so good on biscuits.

So I got to know Tommy from that and other times like combining their corn and playing baseball. He had a neat little house in the country in the center of their black community called The Bottom.

Tommy drove a pickup truck past our house several times a week, and I would know when he was coming. He'd be flying down that clay road in a cloud of red dust, and he'd wave to me with a big smile. I would smile back cause I liked him, but I'd think, "Tommy, that's a little too fast."

Whenever we caught coons, especially with that group, we would give them to Tommy because he was the patriarch of that family. I don't know how old he was at the time. I would guess about seventy. He had white hair, a big smile and a beautiful twinkle in his eyes. He loved to eat coon.   I went hunting with a group of guys from Tommy's clan: a fellow nicknamed Spook, J.B., and a couple of their younger brothers. The very first night, his first season, Waylon treed two coons. Then the next night we got four coons. We got eleven coons with that dog Waylon, this first-year puppy, in the first couple weeks. I'm telling you, he had a reputation, especially in The Bottom. That whole group of people down there in that bottom knew that Waylon, that puppy coon dog, was going to be phenomenal.

My dad didn't live on the farm, he lived in Florida. But he would come up for times of planting and harvesting. He had heard about Waylon. I guess his reputation had spread to Florida. He came up to the farm for a visit and he said, "John, you need to pen that dog up!"

I said, "Dad, I let my dogs run free."

He said, "But I'm gonna want to go coon hunting with him, and he's gonna be worn out. He'll be hunting all day long; he'll be all tired and won't want to hunt at night. You need to pen that dog up, since I'm up here."

Well, you didn't argue with my dad, so I pinned him up. I hated to leave him penned up all day long, but you didn't argue with my dad, so we penned him up. Sometimes I think without the freedom of the Lord, we have our potential penned up.

My brother, Jerry, lived in town in Cairo. We farmed eleven miles north of Cairo. One day, like every day, he came out early in the morning, and he was going to wash out Waylon's pen. So, he turned Waylon out. Waylon took off like a black streak; a black and tan streak, I guess, heading for the woods. To get to the woods you would cross this clay road. As he was crossing this clay road, up the road there was a cloud of dust coming fast. It was Tommy in his pickup truck. Wouldn't you know it, at the time Waylon crossed that road, here came Tommy and WHAM! He ran over Waylon!

That man was so sad about running over that dog. He ran over the dog that was catching him the coons. That dog was famous in their neck of the woods. It was like running over the goose that laid the golden egg. He ran over the famous Waylon. Tommy was so sad, and I think a little bit ashamed. Kind words hardly consoled him that day.

So, I ask you—is that irony? Was that ironic? I'd have to say it was "Dog Gone Irony". There were some strange circumstances involved in that convergence. The decisions made by two patriarchs, one black, one white. Forget the colors. One Black and Tan racing in freedom for his joy in life, and in the blink of an eye, there was a convergence of life and death. Then sadness at the death of a dream of what could have been.

Life is full of swift transitions. It is hard to figure, hard to say. I think, I won't pen anything up, if I can help it. I now live to see other's potential set free.

I am trying to listen to others. I hope I am learning from life. I have come to believe Love is most cool. I wished I could have hugged and held Tommy for a moment of comfort that day; I would have if it wasn't for my own insecurity. I like to think I would today.

I don't think I'll kill any more coons. I don't believe in coincidences, but I do believe in Divine Convergence. I don't understand fully about a lot of things, the true meaning of life; the true meaning of irony. I do believe that moment in time was "Dog Gone Irony." That's the story of Waylon.

In my memory, I can see Waylon running; his long ears flopping back in the wind. Run, Waylon, run.

"It is for freedom that Christ has set us free." Galatians 5:1 NIV

Chapter Fifteen

Blessed are the Peacemakers

This story is set in 1977 in rural southern Georgia. We lived on a farm. We raised cattle and hogs and had a large hog operation. We had 100 brood sows (sows that would raise pigs). We also raised pigs called "feeder pigs" and then fatten them out to a #1 hog. A #1 would weigh between 200 to 220 pounds. We bought feeder pigs to feed, and so we had always about 3,000 feeder pigs on the ground. We would grow and grind the corn to feed them.

We had quite a hog operation, and we also had a cattle operation. We would combine our own corn. We bought a four row Massey Ferguson combine, and one thing I loved to do was to ride that combine in the corn and listen to the ears of corn as they were picked up in the front. The corn would come up a screw-type device that moved them to where the machine would knock the corn off the cob and separate the husks out the back. The corn would hit the side of the "hopper" in there and it would make a loud "Bam Bam" sound when you were really in a good stand of corn. I loved that. Even though it would be a long, dusty day, to me it was pure joy to run that combine.

One time I was running the combine on a field of corn and here comes a young black man. He was walking across the field, and he came up to me. I stopped the combine and told him to come up on it. So, he rode with me and we talked. We were about the same age, and his name was J.B.

J.B. asked me if it would be possible for me to combine his corn. He belonged to a big family of blacks that had quite a bit of acreage in what was called "The Bottom."

We had never combined anybody else's corn for money before and had just started farming about three years earlier. We had a cattle operation in South Florida, and then moved to Georgia. I lived on this farm with my wife Debbie and my son Johnathan, who was just a little boy. So, J.B. asked us to combine his corn, but I didn't know at what price, so I asked him, "What are you being charged?"

He told me, and I said "Well, it sounds like we'd have enough room to make money; but let me just check and see."

As I checked into it, I found that he was probably being charged a premium. I don't know whether it was because he was being taken advantage of as a young black family, but he was being charged a premium. So, I told him I would do it for quite a bit less.

I got to know J.B., his brothers, and some of his other family members, as we combined the corn. In the past, they would drive down a clay road past our farm, but until that time I had never really gotten to know them. I had noticed some black guys playing baseball down in the Bottom. We would go through their farm on the way to our other farm. We had 300 acres on the one farm, and then we would go over maybe 5 miles on a dirt road to our second farm, which had 175 acres of mainly corn. So, I would drive through their farms on this clay road, and that's where I would see them playing baseball.

I was a baseball player. I had played all through school and Little League, junior high, high school, Babe Ruth ball and American Legion Ball. I also played at the University of West Florida on their very first team. Anyway, I loved baseball.

So I asked J.B. about it.

He said enthusiastically, "Come on and play with us."

I thought, "Yeah, that'd be great."

So, one day I drove up there and I began to get to know them. I was the only white guy in the whole black league. The next year my brother played as well.

It was so neat and so country, right down to the names of the teams. One team was called "Coon Bottom," another was called "Dry Springs." The home run fence was made of corn, just like in the movie "Field of Dreams."

By my temperament, I'm somewhat of a phlegmatic. I'm laid-back and I love peace. I don't love peace at any price, but I do love it. I like the concept of being a peacemaker, yet I think it takes the grace of God to bring about peace.

We know that Jesus is called the "Prince of Peace," and sometimes peace comes with a price. When you think about the agony that Jesus suffered--such a tremendous sacrifice-- so that we might have peace with God. He sure wasn't experiencing peace when they tore out His beard or whipped Him with a cat-of-nine-tails until His back was torn up, or spit in His face or stuck a sword in His side. There was no peace in all that violence, and yet He was at peace, for He said, "Father, forgive them, for they know not what they do."

He is the greatest of all peacemakers. The Bible says to seek peace and pursue it and that whenever it is reasonable to be at peace with all men.

Jesus says in the Bible, "Blessed are the peacemakers…"

In this story, I can only give all the glory to God. Sometimes things happen and you find yourself in a dangerous situation. Even though I wasn't going to church at that time, I have to believe that somehow by the grace of God, he used me as a peacemaker.

As usual, we were playing baseball against an opposing team made up of black guys. There was one guy (I won't mention his name as I don't want to hurt his family) who was catching on our team. The most famous and sought-after job in that county baseball league, especially on our team, was what they called "hind-catching." They only used a mask; they didn't use a chest protector or knee guards, shin guards, or even a cup. They had to be so good to get those foul tips. All the young boys were so proud; they wanted to be hind catchers.

This hind catcher was on our team, and as the story was being told to me on the bench, there was bad blood between the hind catcher and another guy on their team because our catcher had had an affair with his wife.

This opposing player was angry, and he was a big guy. He was probably about 6'4". So, they got into it. Their guy had a baseball bat in his hand, and our guy pulled out what was called a "hawk knife." A hawk knife has a curved blade on the end of it, and it's a vicious looking knife. It's a vicious knife to fight with, because if you use that blade to cut, it will cut deeply.

Our guy pulled his knife and I didn't know what to do. I knew I was about to see a potential murder or a real bloodshed, but somehow, by the grace of God, I had peace. I walked up and I stepped in between them. I put my hands out toward each of them and I said something in a calm voice, though I can't remember what exactly I said. I don't know all the dynamics of it; but I really believe it had something to do with the grace of God. Maybe they didn't want the only white guy's blood shed between them, but at about that time the rest of the guys on the teams came up and pulled them apart.

Somebody said, "Let's just play baseball."

Sure enough, we continued the game. I don't know what happened between their bad blood, but that day there was peace on the diamond just because of the grace of God. God used me to be a peacemaker.

I would encourage my heritage, and whoever is reading this, that we would seek peace and that we would be peacemakers in every scene if possible.

"Blessed are the peacemakers: for they shall be called the children of God." Matt. 5:9 KJV

Chapter Sixteen

Run to the Battle

One day, back in the late 1970s, approximately 1977, I was living on a farm near Whigham, Georgia. On this farm we had a lake from which we irrigated our crops. Normally it was a beautiful lake full of bass and bream that were easy to catch especially right before dark. But this day the lake was kinda ugly to look at. We had a drought in 1977. Because of the drought, we had to pump quite a bit of water from the lake to irrigate our okra crop. In fact, the shoreline receded probably ten to fifteen feet below the normal level. The new shoreline looked like red clay.

Also on this farm, we had a Willie's Jeep that we would ride around in. It had a long wheelbase and was kind of old and beat-up. I loved that Jeep. It didn't have a top, so we would put the windshield down and ride around. It felt so good to have that fresh air in your face.

On this particular day, it was about two o'clock in the afternoon, and the wind was blowing unusually hard. We normally didn't have much wind on the farm, but there was a front moving through, and there was a wind blowing steady at about thirty miles an hour.

We had a dam on this farm's lake, and you could drive around the end of the dam. I was riding in that Jeep, going across the end of this dam, and the wind was blowing across the top of the lake so hard that there were actually whitecaps, which was extremely unusual because this was not a big lake. To have whitecaps on that lake, you knew the wind had to be blowing so hard.

It was actually a bluebird day and the sky was bright blue. I looked back over the lake and I saw something out in the lake. I couldn't make out what it was, and I thought, "What is that?" Then I noticed it was a giant snake. It was so big, it was floating up on top of the water and I thought it was an anaconda. No way, it could be an anaconda!

In my own mind, I consider myself about half an expert on snakes. I've been involved with quite a few snakes. I've been in the woods and the swamps so much that I've probably killed at least a dozen rattlesnakes, and probably at least a dozen water moccasins. I've seen copperheads, pigmy rattlers, coral head snakes (which are all poisonous), plus indigo, black snakes, hog snakes and many different snakes. So, I feel like I know snakes. I've studied them a lot in movies, pictures, and books. I knew what anacondas looked like.

This snake was up on top of the water, and it had at least a foot to a foot and a half of its neck up out of the water, swimming along. I think with those whitecaps he was keeping his head up out the waves. This also enlarged the look of the size of it because he was making a wake as he swam across the lake.

I thought, "What is that? Is it a dragon snake, is it an anaconda? It's way too big to be a moccasin."

As I came to a stop, I thought, "Oh my goodness, I have got to kill this snake," because this snake potentially could kill my little boy, or some of the farm animals, like a little pig. It was definitely big enough to kill a man.

I thought, "How in the world am I going to kill this snake?"

I finally got a look at it, and I decided it was the biggest moccasin on God's earth. At about that time, I saw my brother coming. The snake wasn't paying any attention to us. He was fighting the waves. Normally, that size moccasin is very wary and would try to get away from you, although sometimes they say a moccasin is a dangerous snake because he'll come to you. Generally, they will try to get away by going to the water. The water is their element; they can swim under the water. When I've seen them before, they would get away from you by getting in the water and going under the water. They were difficult to kill.

I didn't have a gun with me that day. I looked around, and all I had was what we called a hog stick, or a hog cane. It was a hard, hickory walking cane that might be three feet long. It was used for working hogs, to kind of poke them along and maybe whack them if you had a big sow or boar trying to bite you. All we had was this cane, but that's not a very large object to have between you and the biggest moccasin that ever was. It looked like it was at least six feet long. Most moccasins get short and fat before they get that long. A four-foot moccasin might be as big around as your arm; this snake looked like he was as big around as my thigh, and six feet long.

I thought maybe I could throw something at him, but I might miss. It was really risky to throw something while he was in the water because I didn't know if I could really do damage to him without something solid underneath him.

Then I had the thought that if he was going for the shore, he would have to crawl up that drought-made dry spot between the water and the grass, which was ten or fifteen feet. Then if I could get between him and the water, he would come to the water. That's why I titled this story "Run to the Battle" because I took off with that cane and ran and got between him and the water. I said, "Come to me."

The snake made his last mistake. He froze because he thought he had his head hidden in the grass. With one swift hit with that cane, I smacked him on top of the head, and that stunned him enough so that I could smack him again. Then I pinned his head and cut his head off, because, great-grandchild, if you're ever dealing with a snake, you need to get rid of that head before you grab the tail, because it will curl around on you. Even if he's dead, his body will curl around and strike. My dad taught me to always pin that head and cut it off before you handle it.

So, I cut his head off and then I picked him up. I could not believe how heavy that snake was. He was only five- and one-half feet long, but he was still the biggest moccasin I've ever seen. He was a giant.

God gave me grace to have no fear to get between him and the water. The Bible says, "if God be for you, who can be against you." In that case, I say, "Run to the battle!"

"Do not fear [anything], for I am with you; Do not be afraid, for I am your God. I will strengthen you, be assured I will help you." Isaiah 41:10

Chapter Seventeen

Overcome Evil with Good

Back in 1977, I was running heavy equipment for a road building company near Columbia, Tennessee. I operated a number of different pieces of equipment. My very favorite was called a grader. A grader smooths and cuts in roads and makes them level; it can also cut ditches. A grader is probably one of the hardest ones to master. You had to be a true operator to get it perfectly smooth, but I loved running it.

I also loved running a bulldozer, and I would also run a scraper. The scraper is different from a grader; it hauls dirt. It had to be pushed by a bulldozer to haul dirt.

We would meet early in the morning, sometimes around 5:30, and we had a big fire. We would all talk around that fire before we divided up, loaded up and went off to the job. Many times, we would travel because we were building roads in somewhat distant places.

During this time in my life, I had made a commitment to the Lord and began to follow Him as a disciple. A disciple is defined as a loyal, loving learner of Jesus Christ. A true disciple is a disciple and acts like it 24/7.

I was really trying to be a disciple no matter where I was, which meant on the job. I may not have preached on the job, but every chance I got I would try to witness in some way. If you do that, Jesus said that some of them are going to hate you, because "they hated Me." They hated Jesus. They killed him, they crucified Him for acts of love and wonderful miracles. They crucified Him even though He did no wrong.

Well, if you're going to be His disciple in this world, He said you will have tribulation, or maybe persecution. But He said, "Be of good cheer for I have overcome the world." So, I was trying to be a disciple and was witnessing.

When I would go in on those early mornings, there was one fellow who was an old man. His name was Roy. Roy was older; I was in my twenties and Roy was about seventy.

He was a very grouchy man. I'd heard he had quit drinking, and his wife went to church, but he didn't go to church. He didn't like anything to do with church. He didn't feel well. He was a big, tough, grouchy guy, 6'6" and weighed about 250. He had a big head, a big mustache, and part of a beard. He was always about half-shaved. He would speak in a deep voice and cuss, and just loved to be grouchy about everything.

He took it as his part in life, or his portion in life, to persecute me. He would call me out in front of the other guys. I was young and was fairly new on the job; nobody wants to be called out in a negative way.

He'd say, "John, you think you're a Christian…who are you foolin'? Awww, you're not a Christian. I've seen you drinking, and I've seen you partying. You think you've changed. What makes you think that after all you've done you can be forgiven?"

I was embarrassed, but inwardly I called on the name of the Lord. I said, "Jesus, what do I say?"
The first thing that bubbled out from His Spirit to my spirit was, "Well Roy, I guess love covers my sin."
He could hardly say anything. I noticed he was taken back.
Later I was reading the Bible and I saw the scripture that says, "Love covers a multitude of sins."

Well, that shut Roy up right then, but that was only for a moment. Any time I saw Roy he would try to bring friction. It got worse.

When he was the one running the bulldozer that had to push my scraper, I noticed he was very skillful. He would push my scraper—in fact, it was called picking it up, because he would run up to me real fast, then slow down, lift his blade just a little bit and catch the back of my scraper. If he'd do it just right, very skillfully, I could hardly even feel him pick me up and start pushing the scraper to get a load.

Actually, he was just pushing straight ahead, but he would pick up a little bit. But when he would push me, he would hit the back of my scraper as hard and as fast as he could. It would give me whiplash so bad it would give me a headache. I would have to be pushed by him as many as 50 times in a day. It made me so mad.

One of the iniquities that had been a Newlin trait (that I hope can somehow be broken and not passed on to you) is a little bit of anger. My dad could be an angry man. I'm a proud man. The Newlins, were taught to be proud of that name. It needs to be kept good. A good name, the Bible says, is to be desired. It's valuable, and my dad had a good name. I wanted to have a good name. I was proud of that name, and I was proud of being a man. I thought nobody would intentionally hurt me without a fight.

When he hit my machine with his dozer, it made me so mad I would turn around and look at Roy, and he'd shoot me a bird. Many of you know what that is; almost everybody in America knows what that is. He would give me the finger. Here's a man giving ME the finger, after he just hit me so bad, I got a whiplash? Ohhhh, there would be hot blood running somewhere up my neck and into my ears.
I thought, "I'm gonna kill him. Now how am I gonna kill him? It would be quick and easy with a wrench to the side of the head. Some way or another, I'm gonna kill him."

Then I would remember the Lord. I would say, "Oh Lord, I'm so sorry. I can't kill a man, Lord. You want me to be like you. It says in the Bible that when "You were insulted you insulted not again." "When he was threatened, He threatened not." So, I went to prayer about it. Somehow before I could get back to Roy and try to kill him, the Lord would help me each time.

When I got home, I began to pray. I heard—I think it was in a Sunday sermon, or it may have been in my private Bible time—I saw in Romans 12:21 it says, "Overcome evil with good."

Well, Roy was being evil. So, if I was going to overcome him, according to the Bible, which is what you want to do—you want to do the Lord's will, the Lord's way—then I was going to have to overcome it with good.

I read in Romans 12, where it says, "Then dearly beloved" (speaking to us Christians, from Paul through the Holy Spirit to you), "avenge not yourselves, but rather give place under wrath. For it is written: 'Vengeance is Mine. I will repay,' says the Lord. Therefore, if an enemy is hungry, feed him. If he's thirsty, give him drink. For in so doing thou shalt heap coals of fire on his head. Be not overcome with evil but overcome evil with good."

So I wasn't supposed to take vengeance on Roy. It says, "Give place to wrath." But then it says, "If your enemy is hungry, feed him. If he's thirsty, give him drink." So, I got to thinking. I went by the water cooler, and the whole way I carried a cup of water. I jumped off on Roy's dozer on the tracks, went over and gave him the water. He poured it out. It was starting to make me angry, but I said, "No Lord, help me with this." So, I did it again, and this time he drank it. But he was still acting grouchy toward me.

Then that night at home, I said to my wife Debbie, "Debbie, I want to try to work this plan. I'm going to try to bless Roy. I'm going to overcome evil with good. Would you bake your very best chocolate chip cookies?"

Ohhh, great-grandson or great-granddaughter, if you could only taste Debbie's cookies. I'm telling you, anybody who's ever tasted one of Debbie's chocolate chip cookies with those big chips in there, I'm telling you, they're the best cookies I've ever eaten.

Well, she made me a nice big platter and put it in a Tupperware container for Roy. During the day, I came around and jumped on the tracks of his dozer and gave him those cookies. I actually got kind of a smile, and no more birds from Roy. I would try to relate to Roy, but he was still standoffish.

One day we were in the shop, on a winter day when we weren't running dozers or scrapers. I had a hoe that I had gotten from my landlord. I had a garden in Tennessee that was pretty remarkable. It had corn, pumpkins, tomatoes, squash, green beans, and pole beans. First, I would plant new potatoes and then green peas. It was a big garden, and it really was awesome to eat the vegetables out of it. But I had this hoe, and it was an unusual hoe. It wasn't shaped like most hoes. I treasured that hoe.

Well, I took that hoe to the shop to sharpen it one morning before daylight. It was early. I was sharpening it, and I didn't see Roy slipping over and up behind me. He came up to me and he snatched that hoe out of my hand.

He said, "I want this hoe!" Can you imagine a grown man doing that? He was acting kind of redneck and tough and country. He said, "It's my hoe now! I want this hoe."

He started to walk off, and I said, "Roy, you can't have that hoe. That's my landlord's hoe, and you can't have it."

He said, "What are you gonna do? Take it from me?"

I said, "I might have to."

He started to walk off, and somehow—I don't know how he could let me do it—I took a couple of quick steps and I snatched it back out of his hand. He acted like he was going to come at me, and I acted like I was going to hoe him right between the eyes. He knew it. He backed up.

That wasn't necessarily Christian, but that's what happened with the hoe. I got to praying about it later and I said, "Lord, I'm sorry. But I just didn't feel right about giving him my landlord's hoe. If it was my hoe, I would've given it to him."

Later on, I was working out at my boss' farm. He would work me when the other guys didn't work during the winter, and I had favor with him. One of the reasons I believe I had favor is because I worked really hard. If you'll work hard, you'll have favor. So, he worked me when the other guys didn't work.

I was working out there, and I happened to go in his barn. I looked up on the side of the barn wall, and there was a hoe head like the other hoe that my landlord had. So, I ran to his house, and I said, "Boss, there's an old hoe head that's all rusty up on the side of the barn. I'd like to buy it from you."

He said, "John, you can have that."

I said, "Well, that's great. Thank you very much."

I got it down and took my grinder and polished it up and made it sharp. Then I got a brand-new hickory handle. I couldn't wait. I went into work, and old Roy saw me coming across there. He saw the hoe in my hand.
I said, "Roy, I want to give you something. Here's this hoe." You have never seen a smile go across that big head from ear to ear. It looked like it was 10 inches long, it was so big. He had this big smile. So that right there began to open Roy up.

After that Roy and I worked side by side, and I saw him come to be a Christian. In later days working there, I was Roy's good friend. He would have fought for me. So, there's an example of when somebody's coming really hard against you, they're probably not feeling good. Love them anyway.

"If your enemies are hungry, feed them. If they are thirsty, give them something to drink. In doing this, you will heap burning coals of shame on their heads. Don't let evil conquer you but conquer evil by doing good."
Romans 12:21 NIV

Chapter Eighteen

Can I Pray for Them?

When my son, Johnathan, was eight years old, we were attending a church called The Lord's Chapel near Nashville, Tennessee. Our whole family came to the Lord, and Johnathan, Debbie and I were all baptized on the same day. Johnathan had a simple, childlike faith. He was always pretty bold, even as a child.

One Sunday morning at The Lord's Chapel, as was his custom during the worship time, Pastor would stop and say, "If anyone would like to be healed or have prayer for healing, we'll have you at this time go up to the upper room, and our elders will anoint you with oil and pray for you, and we'll believe for you to be healed according to the scripture."

Johnathan was standing beside me and he said, "Dad, can I go up and pray for them?"

I said, "Well son, if you've got enough nerve to ask the pastor and he says yes, then I would sure say yes."

I didn't think about it anymore during the service. At the end of the service, we were getting ready to leave and I was talking to some people, fellowshipping with them, and I thought, "Now where's Johnathan?" We were fixin' to leave.

I looked around and looked up, and there he was up on the platform talking to the pastor. I made a beeline to him, and when I got there I heard the pastor say, "Well son, why would you want to pray for them?"

Johnathan said, "I believe that if I pray for them Jesus will heal them."

The pastor said, "Well son, next Sunday if you feel faith and you believe that, then I want you to go up there and you can pray for them."

The next Sunday, when the call was made for any sick that wanted to be healed to go to the upper room, Johnathan said, "Dad, can I pray for them."

I said, "Alright."

So we went up to the upper room and he began to pray for a person, and they began to manifest. It's kind of hard to explain what manifest means. Manifest means when something is brought to light or revealed. When he would pray for them, they would get excited. I had never seen anybody manifest. They began to shout and put their hands up and shake. Every one of them claimed to have a healing.

Pretty soon word got out that when Johnathan prayed for people, they got healed. So, the next thing I knew there was quite a few people up there wanting him to pray for them. The next Sunday there was even more people.

Then the next week, we moved to Pensacola, Florida. When we got to Pensacola and found a new church, I didn't feel like it was right to go up to our new pastor and say, "Hey, my son has the gift of healing." I felt like it would be too forward or presumptuous, or maybe I was just too shy. I never did feel comfortable with that, so I never said anything.

I never really saw Johnathan pray for anybody else. I did see him lead a couple kids to the Lord in Pensacola. But I never really saw him pray for other people after that.

Later, when we were at Brownsville Assembly of God, there was a speaker that came. She was said to be a prophetess, and she could hear a word from the Lord for people. That night there was about a thousand people there, she called out a couple people to come to the platform, and Johnathan was one of them.
She said, "Oh...the Lord shows me that you have healing in your hands." So once again it was confirmed.

Johnathan loves music. He used to sing in church when he was young, and later. He has a gift to write songs; he has written quite a few songs. He has a C.D. of songs. But he also, I believe, has the gift of healing.

These days, he's a chiropractor, laying his hands on people every day that he works. I'm just very proud of my son Johnathan. Even as I say it here in writing, I just want him to know that I believe he is a great man. It's not about how big you are, how fast you are, or how much money you have. You see, I'm very proud of his integrity and his character.

I just believe the Lord is going to use Johnathan more in the way of healing than we've ever seen. I believe there's healing in his hands. In my mind, I can hear him asking the Lord....... "Can I pray for them?"

"They will be able to place their hands on the sick, and they will be healed." Mark16:18 NLT

Chapter Nineteen

So You Want Faith

In 1979, I had just come back to the Lord. I started going to a church called The Lord's Chapel. I was hungry, very hungry. I would go to church on Sunday morning, Sunday night, and Tuesday night. I would drive 35 miles one way to go. This story really starts when we had a guest speaker on a Tuesday night. The guest speaker was named Holy Hubert.

Brother Hubert (I had and still do have great respect for him) didn't call himself Holy Hubert, but other people called him Holy Hubert because of the things he said and did. He had memorized the New Testament and the Psalms and was considered a Bible scholar and a preacher.

At this time when he was speaking at The Lord's Chapel, he was 65 years old. He spoke with a strong confident voice. It was my custom to sit down on the front row; I was hungry.

The Lord had just begun to clean me up. Not that it matters how you look, but I had long hair and a beard and looked pretty rough. Most of the other people there looked like church people; they didn't look like me. So, I was sitting on the front row, listening to Brother Hubert tell some of his stories of what had happened to him in the Lord.

I call them exploits in the Lord. Somewhere in the Bible it talks about an exploit. To me, an exploit in the Lord is where the Lord uses you in ministry to bring about fruit for the Kingdom. It's usually where God used a person in an unusual way.

Well, Hubert had these exploits he was talking about and it was very interesting to me. In one of them, he said he was in California and there was a large convention of Hell's Angels. They were having a big Hell's Angels outdoor party convention, with a big stage. There were thousands of bikers that arrived there. They were playing music, and all kinds of pagan things were going on.

Hubert somehow slipped up onto the Hell's Angels platform and took the microphone and started to preach Jesus. As soon as they realized what he was doing, they grabbed him and pulled him off the back of the stage and began to hit him right in the mouth and the nose. Every time they would hit him, he would look at them and say, "I love you in Jesus." He could barely speak through the blood and they would hit him again, and he would say, "I love you in Jesus."

Hubert said they dragged him off and he lived. A couple years later, in the middle of the night, on his front door he heard, BAM! BAM! BAM! He went to the door and opened it, and here was one of those Hell's Angels.
He said, "Ohhhh, I finally found you! It's been two years and I've been tormented! I need to know this Jesus! I couldn't believe that as I hit you in the face you told me you loved me. Tell me about this Jesus!"

So Hubert told him about Jesus and the plan of salvation and led him into salvation. That biker man became a powerful evangelist. He has a biker ministry and has seen many, many people come to the Lord.

In that example, I call that an exploit. Hubert had really paid the price to see fruit in the Kingdom. It's my prayer, it's my hope, it's my desire, it's my purpose for writing this book, is that my heritage and others will come to know this God that I love and serve.

Hubert told other stories, and some were almost too strange to tell. He changed the subject and looked down at me in the front row, and said, "Young man, do you want faith?"

At that time I was just too shy to hardly even look at him, so I didn't say anything and kind of looked down. He said, "No! I'm talking to you, young man. Look up here at me. I'm asking you—do you want faith?"

If you push me, I can get bold. I looked him in the eyes, and I said, "Yes."

He said, "Well, young man, if you want wisdom, then go to the book of Proverbs and study those proverbs and meditate on them. I guarantee you; you'll get wisdom. If you want to know about love you can study places like I Corinthians 13 where it talks to you about love; you can study that and learn how to walk in love. But I'm asking you—do you want faith?" He said, "Son—and the rest of you—if you want faith, meditate on the Messianic prophecies."

I just wasn't sure what a Messianic prophecy was at that time. He began to explain a little bit about them, and in this short chapter of this book I'm not sure I'd be able to totally explain to you a Messianic prophecy. In fact, I have a book that will soon be coming out (I say soon by faith) that's going to be titled "So You Want Faith?" In that book I want to delve extensively into this subject.

Hubert went on to explain that Jesus is the light to the Gentiles and Paul was an apostle of Jesus' light to the Gentiles. Gentiles are anybody who is not Jewish. Paul said, "I can prove to you that Jesus is the Christ through looking through the scriptures and understanding the scriptures."

Well, the scriptures Paul was talking about were not the New Testament as we see Jesus in red letters, and His words, and the gospels about Jesus, where we come to understand Him. The scriptures he was talking about were the Book of the Law, Jewish Mosaic books of the law, the Book of Psalms, and the prophets. So, we're talking about a Messianic prophecy. The Messianic part is a root word for the Messiah. The Jews were looking for the Messiah. They were looking for Him to come, they just didn't understand that He came, and they knew Him not. Jesus is the Messiah.

They didn't have that understanding. Some came to the revelation and believed, but most of the Jewish scribes were looking for a time and place for Him to come as a great king of kings. They understood that there were Messianic prophecies. They were looking for the coming of this great anointed one from God.

I want to give you some examples of Messianic prophecies. Hubert went on to tell a story about a time that he had a type of a debate, a discussion, with a Jewish scribe that was supposed to be a scribe of scribes; the top notch, best Jewish scribe. Hubert, in the same sense, is a type of a scribe for a Christian. He's such a scholar, somebody that studies the Word.

He invited this Jewish Rabbi over to his house and they

started a discussion in the early evening. Hubert was believing that the Lord would reveal to this man that Jesus is the Messiah. He said he began to explain to him the scriptures. This scribe was so well versed in the scriptures and had his own ideas on them that every time Hubert would share a scripture the scribe would say, "Yes, that stands for David, Hubert. Don't you understand that it's speaking of King David, a root of Jesse? It's speaking of King David."

Hubert said that if he didn't know that doubt was sin, he would have sinned. He would have come to the point of doubt because this scribe was so strong in his explanation. He said it was way late in the morning, two o'clock in the morning, and he finally had just about had it. He cried out to God. He was frustrated. He got in the middle of his living room floor, knelt down on his knees, put his hands up and cried unto God. He said, "Oh God! Oh, Holy Spirit, please give me the scripture that this man will understand that You are the Messiah." He said that just as clear as anything, he heard very strongly Genesis 49:10. It's a Bible verse. Genesis chapter 49, verse 10, about halfway through the verse, the Spirit says, "A scepter shall not depart, nor a lawgiver from between his feet, until Shiloh come."

The scribe recognized something in that verse, and he said, "You know Hubert, it's late. Let me meditate on this and get back to you."

Three days later the scribe called Hubert and said, "Hubert, no longer call me Rabbi. Call me brother."

I'm sure that as Hubert was witnessing all these other scriptures it was ministering to this Rabbi, but this one, I think, was the one that broke the camel's back, so to speak. In Genesis 49:10 when he was talking about the scepter, he was talking about the One who had the authority. The lawgiver also had to do with the priest. He said the scepter would not depart until Shiloh comes. So, the scribe looked at this prophecy from a geographical perspective and knowing the scepter (the place of power) had already departed the land i.e. Jerusalem. He also looked at it chronologically. This same scripture says, "until Shiloh come." The Jewish Rabbi recognized that when that scepter departed, in that verse speaking of Shiloh, meant that the Messiah had already come. It meant so much to that Rabbi, and it means so much to me. It proves that Jesus is the Messiah.

Scholars say that there are over 300 Messianic prophecies that speak of the Messiah. Jesus said over and over that He must fulfill what is written in the scriptures. God says it's the glory of God to hide a matter; it's the glory of man to seek it out, to find it. It's like a treasure that's hidden.

Another example of a Messianic prophecy is when Isaiah wrote in Isaiah 53. It speaks of a suffering servant. It talks about a Lamb that goes to slaughter and opens not His mouth. It speaks of Him being wounded for our transgressions and bruised for our iniquities, and the chastisement of our peace was put upon Him.

So the best way to interpret Bible is with Bible. Later on, in the New Testament, as Phillip the disciple of Jesus had just been in a great revival, it said he was translated to another location, or it sounds like he was just found immediately in another location. I don't know that I understand that, and it's hard for my faith to believe he was translated through time and space. But that's the way many interpret it. Anyway, Phillip found himself next to a chariot, and there was a man in the chariot that is known as the Ethiopian eunuch. This man was reading in the scripture.

Phillip says, "Do you understand what you're reading?"
The eunuch said, "How can I? It's talking about this suffering servant."

That man was reading Isaiah 53. So, Phillip got up on the chariot with him and began to explain to him Jesus. The light bulb came on in the eunuch's mind and he believed it was Jesus.

He said, "What keeps me from being baptized?" And he did get baptized. The Ethiopian Eunuch received the revelation from the scripture pointing to Jesus in Isaiah 53.

I say to you, my heritage and to anyone who reads this book, "So You Want Faith?" Meditate on the Messianic prophecies and you'll have great faith.

Chapter Twenty

The Prophetic Dream: What Does It Mean?

When we were living in Spring Hill, Tennessee, I became a Christian and I was hungry for the Lord. As I said before, in another story, I would go to church on Sunday mornings, Sunday nights, and then I would go to church on Tuesday night. The name of the church we attended was called The Lord's Chapel. It was near Nashville, Tennessee, and it was about a thirty-five-mile drive to the Lord's Chapel.

I began looking for a place to worship and get fed the Word of God on a Wednesday night because The Lord's Chapel didn't meet on Wednesday night. Like I said, I was hungry for the Word of God. I still am! I knew somewhere there would be a Wednesday night meeting. I had looked just about everywhere in Spring Hill and it seemed like the churches I visited were dry or I couldn't relate.

Finally, this guy I was working with named Red said, "Come on John, come to my church. We're having revival every night." I'm pretty conservative in certain ways, and I thought, "every night, are you kidding me?" Well, rather than take Debbie down there to check it out, I thought, "I'll go visit

Red's church on a Wednesday night and see by myself."

At this point I must digress. About a month earlier, I had a dream that I knew was a God Dream. You say, John, how do you know it was a God Dream? Well, you just know…when it's about God, for one thing. Solomon in the Bible says dreams are about the "multitude of business of things." You go through the day and you see a bunch of things and do a bunch of things, and it rolls through your mind at night. That's what you call just a normal dream. Don't put a lot of stock in those. But when it's a God Dream it's different. The Bible is full of men and women having dreams, especially men having dreams having something to do with God; maybe being visited by an angel, or God spoke to them through a dream.

Well, I had such a dream. I was sleeping and began dreaming in the middle of the night. To this day, I remember the dream vividly and in detail. I believe this is one sign that this is a God Dream. I'm going to go in detail in the retelling of the Dream because later in the future, I experience what happened in the dream to the same detail. That's why I call it prophetic. What happened in the Dream happened in reality later in the future.

In this particular dream, I went into the back of a church, and noticed there were three sections. The church had a section in the middle and two aisles on either side of a middle section. In my dream I walked into the back of the church and I thought, "Hmm…where am I going to sit?" I decided to go to the right aisle, three quarters of the way from the back, maybe just a quarter of the way in from the back door, and then sit in the middle section. I did that, and I noticed that the platform was a golden brown. A preacher was on the platform preaching. I noticed a lady with a bun over to my right, and a little girl. All of a sudden, everybody in the church, by the direction of the pastor, began to jump up and down with their hands up. I was fairly new to the charismatic movement and I had seen some people raise their hands. I had seen a couple of people seem like they jumped a little, but I had never seen the whole congregation jumping up and down with their hands up in the air, all of them. I looked over and the little old lady with the bun, she was jumping up and down, and I saw the little girl jumping up and down.

Then I looked over to the left, at the front of the church, I saw a little bald man. He started walking up the other far aisle and came around the back, and he came to me (this is still in the dream, now). He put his hands up underneath my shoulder blades from the back, and he gave me like a lift-off, like I was going to jump. When I did jump up, in the dream, we all went right on up, through the ceiling and the roof, into the sky. I looked down and saw how the earth was getting further away, and I had my hands up. All of a sudden, I got a shot of adrenaline. In my dream it was such a thrill, but in reality, there in my bed, I got a shot of something into my heart. In the dream, and even as I was waking up, it was like, "Whoooooooooooaaaaaaaa…." It was the most incredible rush I had ever had in my whole life.

I woke up and I told Debbie, "Debbie, I just had a God dream." At that time, she was sleeping so hard and she didn't really want to hear it right then. Later on, we began to think more about dreams. We actually ask each other every morning, "Did you have any dreams?" and we talk about our dreams. But at this time, she didn't really want to hear about it. I think I told her the next morning, but I kind of put the whole thing on the side. I thought, "My goodness, it had something to do with the rapture," but I didn't know what.

It was about a month after I had the dream when Red asked me to go to his church. On a Wednesday night, I went there by myself and I walked into the back of the church and I thought, "Whoa…this is like what Yogi Berra said, 'This is like déjà vu all over again.'" I thought, "I have been here before." I began to look where I was going to sit. I went over to the right aisle and I sat about three-quarters of the way back, in the center, in that same area as in the dream. I looked over and there was the lady with the bun. Then I saw the little girl down to the right. Then a little bit later in the service, the pastor directed everybody, the whole congregation to raise their hands, and they all began to jump up and down. He called it "jumping for joy."

I looked over to the left, down in front, and there was the little bald man. He came back around, just like he did in the dream, came up the left aisle, came around behind me. When he came to me, he didn't touch me under both shoulder blades; he touched me under one shoulder blade. I had my hands up and everyone else was jumping up and down. Here's what he said: "Won't you come dance with us men?"

I noticed on the far-left side there was a group of young men dancing. Like I said, I was kind of new to the charismatic or Pentecostal-type service and I felt a little uncomfortable. But I knew this was just like the dream, and perhaps what he was saying was a word of wisdom. The dream was a word of knowledge. Many times, in the Bible people would be contacted by God with a word of knowledge and then be led to somebody with a word of wisdom. I didn't know it at the time, but after studying the Bible, I've seen a word of wisdom follow a word of knowledge.

I knew to go with him. So, we went toward the back and

around to that far left side, and the young men were dancing to the Lord. They would twirl and spin, and twirl and roll around some until they got dizzy. They were having such a good time. I couldn't quite step into it. I tried to move my feet a little bit, but I didn't feel comfortable. It was out of my comfort zone to be thinking about dancing in the front of a church.

I left that service and thought many, many times on what that dream actually meant. I believe it was prophetic. I had the dream first and then it happened—how could that be? I knew it had to do with God, because it was in a church and it had to do with God.

The Lesson

I believe the lesson or the reason for the dream is found in the interpretation. The answer is twofold. Here's the way I have interpreted it. Joy is an excellent emotion; it's really the best emotion. Over and over in the Bible it says, "Rejoice, and again I say rejoice." Jesus said, "Hey, I want your joy to be full." In the dream and in the church the people were jumping for joy. The young men were dancing with great joy. So, I believe that dancing unto the Lord is one way to separate yourself unto the Lord so that you're able to praise Him through a dance. It's worship through a dance. The Bible says, "Love the Lord thy God with all thy heart, with all thy might, with all thy strength." Some people say, "Well, yeah…but you can't just dance like that, you'd need to be under the unction of the Spirit." But I say, I've seen in the Bible where David says, "I will clap my hands." Well, that comes from his will. So, I say, "I will dance unto the Lord." If I can get past worrying about the person on my left and the right, I can dance unto the Lord. If I can just, with all my might, with all my heart, put my mind on the Lord and be free to dance unto Him, it takes me to a place of joy. It's like jumping for joy.

That's my understanding of that dream. If you think you have a better interpretation, please write me. If you see me jumping for joy or dancing in church, I'm just being obedient to the heavenly vision. Can you really know or see something before it happens? You can through a God dream. He has turned my mourning into joy. At least that's been the experience with God by this ordinary man.

"And David danced before the Lord with all his might." 2 Samuel 6:14 KJV

"Then shall the virgin rejoice in the dance, both young men and old together: for I will turn their mourning into joy, and will comfort them, and make them rejoice from their sorrow." Jeremiah 31:13 KJV

Chapter Twenty-one

Dip It in the Muddy Water

This story occurred after I had come back to the Lord, in about 1980. I was pretty much a brand-new Christian. I began to believe the things of the Lord by faith, one of them being that the Lord can heal. There's a scripture that says, "These signs shall follow them that believe," and one of the signs is, "They shall lay hands on the sick and they shall recover."

Well, I am a disciple. A disciple means to be a loyal, loving learner of Jesus. A disciple wants to know Jesus more. He wants to walk with Him and follow in His steps. A true disciple wants to be obedient to Him; and wants to hear Him and obey Him.

I'm not saying I'm a perfect disciple, but when you look at the early disciples, they weren't perfect either, especially Peter. I can thank the Lord for Peter's example because I'm a lot like him, in that I make a lot of mistakes. I say things that I shouldn't say. But Peter did have faith, unusual faith. He had stories, stories about an ordinary man's experience with God.

This story has to do with a healing that I saw happen as the Lord used me. Once again, I've said it in this book a number of ways. I really want to give the credit and the glory to the Lord.

Everybody has weaknesses, and my biggest one is that I'm full of myself. The self is really an enemy to God. We need to crucify ourselves daily. You know what they say about pride: it's like bad breath; everybody else knows you have it, but you don't. My problem is that I know that I've got it, but I need to do something with my pride all the time. Like repent, humble myself before the living God. Recognize He is great, and I am small. Basically, he is God and I'm not. I am just a man, but His man, His servant, His disciple. It is His Spirit, and His healing.
So, here's a story about healing. Oh, I don't want to act like it's something that I did. It was just by the grace of God, and by believing His Word, and trying to do His will. I saw the Lord heal a man.

As this story unfolds, I was working building roads in Tennessee. I was a scraper operator at that time. We were building some roads about fifty miles from our home base, and we were just finishing up the job. The road was finished, and we were about to move our scrapers back home.

It is a glorious day when you get to run your scraper on the highway, especially on the interstate. Running really fast with no brakes, through the mountains of Tennessee, the only thing stopping you was if you just barely touched your scraper blade down to the road. We were always so afraid we would dig in and tear the road up, but we never did. You just had to be careful not to burn up your blade because it would get so hot from touching the road when you had to stop.

This story started out in the morning of the move. My best buddy on the job was a fellow named Red. Red was working there when we were getting ready to leave with our scrapers, but the boss wanted Red to cut some rebar that was down in a hole. You cut rebar with a very hot blow torch. It had been raining, and there was a mud puddle down in this hole. It was probably about eight feet down there where Red was working. Somehow, when he was working, he slipped, and the blow torch went across the end of his fingers. He screamed and began to holler, and he said, "Call John! Call John! Call John!" He wanted me to pray for him.

They called me, and I went running and leaped down there into the hole. He said, "Oh John, I put the blow torch across my hand!"

I said, "Let me see." I looked at it, and his fingernails looked like fried chicken. I've been around a lot of cuts and wounds, and burns, so I knew what I was looking at. It was a bad burn.

I said, "Red, we've got to pray. We've got to ask the Lord how to pray."

Strangely enough, something came to my mind. You say, "John, did the Lord tell you?" I don't know. I believe that it came from His Spirit to my spirit, to my soul, which is your mind, will and emotions. I heard a strange thing, or at least I thought I heard a strange thing.

I said, "Red, we're going to do a thing of faith. Dip that burnt hand down in that muddy water. Now we're going to believe like when the Lord told Naaman to dip in the muddy waters of the Jordan and he would be healed. Let's dip it seven times." I also laid hands on him and prayed healing in the name of

Jesus.

So he did. He dipped it seven times in the muddy water. He came up and I said, "Let's get you to a doctor if you want to."

He said, "I'm believe by faith that I'm healed, John. I believe by faith I'm healed."

At about that time, it was time to load 'em up and head down the road. Red kept that hand curled up, and he drove that scraper with one hand all the way back to the shop. He and I never looked at it, we never said one thing about it.

I said, "You going to church tonight?"

He said, "You better believe it."

I said, "I'll see you there."

I went to his church at that time. It was in revival. The revival ran for quite a long time. This was just a little church in Tennessee, but they would have revival every night. So, we went, and I saw Red at that revival meeting. We both sat on the front row.

I said, "Red, what about that hand?"

He opened it up and said, "John, it's like baby's skin. Look at it." I looked at it, and it was all pink and pretty and didn't hurt him.

I said, "Let's just give glory and praise to the Lord because we've seen a true healing." I was normally shy about raising my hands in church. That night it was so easy to raise my hands and praise the Lord during the worship song service.

If you see me raising my hands to praise the Lord, perhaps I'm remembering the day the Lord said, "Dip It In The Muddy Water."

"So Naaman went down to the Jordan River and dipped himself seven times, as the man of God had instructed him. And his skin became as healthy as the skin of a young child, and he was healed!" 2 Kings 5:14 NLT

Chapter Twenty-Two

Jailhouse Prayer

I had a friend that I worked with in Tennessee named Red. You may have already heard of him in some of the other stories. He was a wild one; he had long red hair and a bright red beard, with lots of freckles. He was wiry and tough, and real countrified. We both got saved at about the same time.

We both ran scrapers. Red was probably the best scraper operator I've ever known or heard of; he was unbelievable. There's a big difference between hauling dirt with a scraper and operating a scraper, and knowing how to do it, as far as digging ditches and cutting grade with one.

Red got saved, but he had a pretty wild past life before he got saved. He had been busted for drugs, specifically coke. We became great friends. We shared the gospel at work and went to church together sometimes. With his past transgressions, there were consequences. There are always consequences to sin.

He was so worried that he had to go before the court. I told him, "Red, tell them your testimony. Tell them you're changed and that you're not going to do that anymore. Ask the judge if he would have mercy and tell him that you will be an excellent citizen."

I really believe Red meant it, and when he went before the judge, he told him that. He still got some time. He had to go serve weekends in the Polanski Jail, which was probably sixty miles from where we lived. I guess Red had gotten busted down that way. He just hated to go to jail because he felt like his life had changed. It had been a year since he had done any drugs or drank whiskey. We had been in a revival and he went about every night. I believe Red was a changed man.

One weekend I went down to that jail to visit Red. I didn't know what to expect. He was in a small jail cell, but there was about half a dozen other guys in there. I wasn't on the inside of the cell, I was on the outside of the bars, just me. I think there were about six or seven guys, including Red on the inside of the bars. Those guys were making fun of us sharing the gospel. One of them said, "Alright buddy, if you believe God, why can't you pray to your God and have Him deliver Red out of this jail?"

I kind of liked that. I hated that he was dissing God, but I kind of liked that he was. So many times, I've seen in the Bible that when somebody disses (disrespects) God, and you're there for God, God will show up on your behalf. So, I took it as a challenge. I said, "Alright, right here before us, I'm going to call out to Almighty God and ask Him to deliver Red and leave you guys here in jail."

Red and I grabbed hands and prayed out loud, eyes open. I prayed a prayer that seemed like it had great faith. I said, "God, to show these men that you're God, and because

Red has changed his life for the way of doing right, I pray that You would deliver him out of this jail, right here, right now."

We prayed that prayer, and just when we barely got done with it, all of a sudden we heard over the speakerphone, "Red, report to the front." deputy came and got Red out. They cut him loose and he never had to go back. They brought him out of jail right then, right there.

Now I don't know if there was some kind of microphone, where that guy up front heard that. I don't think so. I don't think he would have had that kind of authority to do it. It must have been in the works, but we didn't know it was in the works. We did not know that guy was coming right then. You should have seen the looks on those guys' faces. Hey, you should've seen the looks on mine and Red's face. So, I say, call to the Lord, and He will deliver you.

That day, He answered our "Jailhouse Prayer."

Chapter Twenty-Three

The Too Tight Boots That the Lord Gave Me

Back in 1979, I was a brand-new Christian. I was learning things about becoming a Christian. I was going to church all the time and I was reading books about the faith.

I read a book by Charles Capps that was about praying and being specific in your requests, naming exactly what you're believing for. In fact, I saw a scripture where Jesus spoke, "Whatever you desire when you pray, believe that you receive it and you shall have it."

In those days I wasn't making a lot of money, probably about seven dollars an hour. For a family, just one income of seven dollars an hour was not a lot of money in America. Debbie and Johnathan had needs, and I put their needs ahead of my needs. I was even embarrassed sometimes when I would go down to the altar to pray and I had a hole in the bottom of my shoe. I would somehow try to fix my foot so that nobody could see it.

I did have a desire, a new pair of cowboy boots. Back

when I was cowboying, one thing that was really nice in life was a good pair of cowboy boots, a pair that would fit you just right. I never liked them where they were too sharp on the front, but I didn't like them too rounded off either. To tell you the truth, you need them somewhat sharp on the front to get them in and out of a stirrup really easy. If the boots were made right and fit right, they just felt great.

So, I had just read this idea about praying and being specific. I tried a "specific" prayer.
I said, "Lord, I want a pair of black cowboy boots. I know how they look, and You know how they look; not too sharp on the front. I'd like them to be leather all the way by the soles, leather bottoms, leather tops." I prayed that way specifically and then I told Debbie, "I prayed specifically for these boots, I want you to agree with me."

Three days later, Debbie's aunt came over to her mother's house. Debbie had not told her mother about our prayer; we hadn't told anybody. Her aunt said, "Frances, do you think John could wear these new black boots? I know they're too big for Curtis (my father-in-law). They're a size 10 and they're just too small for Peddeley (Debbie's uncle) to wear, he couldn't even put them on. We bought them up in Tennessee and we can't take them back. Would you see if John could wear them?"

Honest to God, they were exactly the boots I prayed for. But when I first put them on they were a little tight, but I still said they were great. I knew they were the boots the Lord gave me. Even if they were a little tight, I was going to break them in.
For the first few weeks Debbie and I would laugh because she'd say, "How are those boots?"

I'd say, "Awww, they're gonna be alright, they're gonna stretch out." But we joked about them. We called them the too tight boots that the Lord gave me. For the first couple weeks I walked around with sore feet, but when they finally got broken in they were the best pair of boots I ever had. I wore them for years and years. I have never had such a comfortable pair of boots.

I think the lesson is, yes, you should pray specifically. Sometimes it may not be exactly like you think it should be, but you hang in there with the Lord and it'll fit.

Just like: "The Too Tight Boots That The Lord Gave Me."

"I tell you, you can pray for anything, and if you believe that you've received it, it will be yours." Mark 11:24 NLT

Chapter Twenty-Four

Deliverance at Revival

One night at the Brownsville Revival, I was on the platform as the prayer team coordinator. Each night after the worship and the preaching of the Word, the evangelist, Steve Hill, would call for repentance with an altar call. Afterward, we almost always had a time of prayer ministry. My job was to coordinate the prayer team.

There were a lot of things happening at revival that some people wouldn't understand. The main emphasis of the revival was about lifting up Jesus and souls getting saved. Sometimes people that had demons would manifest, which means the demons would reveal themselves. We had a team that worked in the deliverance ministry, but we called them the "Personal Ministry Team" so that people wouldn't get offended. They might get labeled a demoniac, if we said, "This person needs deliverance" and it was overheard by someone that didn't understand. We had people coming to the revival from all different kinds of churches, from all around the world, and some people didn't know what to think about the deliverance ministry. Hey, to be honest, I am not sure I understand deliverance.

The prayer team, the ushers, and anyone else would come to me if somebody needed deliverance, and I would direct them to the Personal Ministry Team. Then they would get with that person, and if they felt like it really was demonic, they would have permission to take the person back to a room and pray for deliverance, if that's what the person wanted.

On this night, a prayer team member came to me and said, "John, you'd better come quickly. We've got somebody who definitely needs personal ministry." Debbie (my wife) and I had been on the platform, and it was a time of prayer with a lot going on. I went with the prayer team member and there was a beautiful young blonde girl, about sixteen years old. As I walked up, her mother was saying, "What's wrong with my baby? What's wrong with my baby?"
This was a perfect example for the need to be discreet and diplomatic, because her church group had come from a Church of Christ somewhere in the country. They couldn't believe this girl was now growling like a dog. When I looked at her, her eyes were rolled all the way back in her head and she was growling, snarling, showing her teeth and shaking her head back and forth.

Her mother kept saying, "What's wrong with my baby?"
I said, "Ma'am, we have a personal ministry team that would be glad to pray with her and try to help her, and you would be able to go with her. Would you like to do that?"
She said, "I sure would." The personal ministry team came and took the young girl and her mom to a private room.

Sometime during the prayer time (which might have lasted a couple hours although it never seemed that long), all of a sudden I saw the young girl and her mother back in the service, and here was this girl—her face was shining. Her eyes were normal and shining, she had a big smile and her hands were up. She was praising God. Her mother and the whole group were just praising God until the end of the service.

It just seemed plain as day to me that she had been delivered of a demon, and now she was worshiping the Lord. Those were special moments at revival. I call them Brownsville moments. There were so many precious moments that happened during the revival, I think I should write a book about it.

For now, this memory, I call... Deliverance at Revival.

Chapter Twenty-Five

What are You Going to Do When You're Faced with Death?

Back in 1979, we moved from our farm in South Georgia to a small town just south of Nashville Tennessee. My first job after we arrived was with a construction company that specialized in excavation and building roads. I operated heavy equipment building roads. I had operated heavy equipment earlier in my life when I had worked at my dad's quarry, so I knew I could run heavy equipment. I took a job with them and eventually was promoted to running a scraper. A scraper is a big earth-moving piece of equipment, and these particular scrapers had to be pushed with a bulldozer to pick up a load of dirt.

We built roads all over Tennessee, but most of the roads were fairly close to Nashville. Running a scraper was an unusual job. They were big and loud, and somewhat dangerous. They could run forty miles an hour with twenty tons of dirt, but there were no brakes. You had to control how you stopped by barely touching your blade, which is in the middle of the machine, down to scrape up dirt. If you were really good with it, you could do fine detail finish work on a road or move large loads of rock, dirt, or clay.

On one particular job we were repairing a dam about a hundred miles south of Nashville. We would get our load of clay from a borrow pit on the top of the mountain. Then we would race down a very steep road down to the bottom of the mountain. We would dump our load there, at the base of this dam. We had dug out a place at the bottom of the dam where it was leaking a little bit. We would put that clay down at the bottom and it would be packed in there with earth-packing machines.

A scrapper operator would make about thirty loads a day. Get your load up top and then race down the mountain. You would just barely touch your scraper pan to the road as you went down, and it would keep the road really smooth. Then we would have to go back up a ramp onto the dam, and then back up the hill.

I had a very exciting life-threatening incident there. One particular day it was raining, and that meant the clay would get very slippery. It was too steep. It was just too slick. Good operators improvise. We would have to turn our machines around and back our pans or scrapper up this ramp, and the ramp wasn't much wider than our scraper. The only way to get traction was to turn around and back up this ramp. When you got to a certain point the road narrowed even more on the dam and became like a cliff off the edge of the dam, and it was a hundred-foot drop with a bunch of jagged rocks at the bottom. We were either very brave or very foolish operators. It was extremely dangerous.

Everybody took pride in being a good scraper man. Some could operate the machine better than others, and the highest level was to be called an "Operator", instead of just a "dirt hauler". You never wanted to make a mistake, especially one where you had to shut down somebody else's job to come help you with the dozer.

On this day it was raining harder and harder. We should've knocked off, but the boss wasn't there at that point to give us permission to quit. So, we kept trying to work, hauling loads. We had to back up this ramp and it got so slippery that one time as I was backing up my scraper started to slide. I should've stopped right there and gotten help from Roy, the dozer man, because my machine had started to slide off the edge.

I wanted to get out of the predicament on my own. I was full of pride, and definitely didn't want to have to go get old Roy to help me basically get unstuck. I was in a precarious position, right on the edge of the cliff, and the more I tried to get unstuck on my own, the more my scraper would slide over to the edge of that cliff. I am reminded of a famous movie line where George Clooney says, "We're in a tight spot, boys!" Yes, I was in a tight spot!

I finally worked myself to where I was in terrible shape, right on the edge of the cliff. I had to get word to Roy, so I sent somebody to go get him. You see, I couldn't get off my machine or I would lose it. He came with his dozer and they got a big cable and hooked it to it. I had to operate my machine and as he began to pull with his dozer and I began to maneuver, I slipped a little further. My heart went up in my throat. Then his cable broke. My scraper, from the force of the cable breaking, actually slid out and was teeter-tottering. My cab in the front of the machine where I operated it was hanging out over this cliff, and I was teeter-tottering. It looked like any second it would be going over the cliff and I would be crashing a hundred feet below on these rocks.

In the meantime, quite a crowd of co-workers had gathered, and they were watching. One of my best friends, Gill, was over on the dam, not far from me. He was up on the dam and I was on the edge of the cliff. He was a Christian and put his hands together like he was praying for me. I made the same sign back to him.

You would have thought that I would have been afraid, but I had become a Christian—and not just a Christian, a radical Christian. The way I describe a radical Christian is someone who loves Jesus more than you. Somebody who's not a Christian might think that's kind of funny, but someone who is a Christian will understand. We ought to love Jesus with all our heart. It's one of God's commandments that we love Him with all our might, with all of our strength, and that we love our neighbor as ourselves. We ought to love one another.

The situation I found myself in reminds me of the scripture found in Psalms 34, and it says, "I sought the Lord and He heard me, and He delivered me of all my fears."

Soooo, as I teeter-tottered over certain death, I looked opened-eyed up at the raining sky and called on the Lord. At this particular moment, rather than being so afraid that I might panic, scream or shake, instead, the Presence of the Lord came upon me. I could feel Him! I was facing death right at that moment. I began to sing a song. It was a song of deliverance. The song, to me, was like an offering from me to the Lord. I had perfect peace. To have perfect peace in a moment like that is just short of a miracle.

Thank God, Ol Roy quickly hooked two cables to me

and another dozer cabled to his dozer and they snatched me off the cliff's edge. The rescue was anticlimactic, but we surely did rejoice! Ol Roy was speechless. Gil was a very conservative Church of Christ man. That day he jumped and praised God like a Pentecostal. I had peace but a touch of aftershock. I couldn't thank God enough. Actually, still can't.

So I ask you: "What are you going to do when you face death? If you're riding in an airplane and it starts to go down because the engine quits, are you going to scream out and be afraid and panic? Or are you going to praise the Lord?"

That day, at the moment I thought I might die, the Lord gave me a song, one we had sung in church. It goes like this:
"Unto Thee O Lord

Do I lift up my soul…

Unto Thee O Lord

Do I lift up my soul…

O my God

I trust in Thee

Let me not be ashamed

Let not mine enemies triumph over me."

So, I say to you, great-grandchild or friend, whoever happens to be reading this, "You don't have to be afraid, if you know the Lord, no matter how perilous the situation. What are you going to do? Maybe the better question is ...Do you know the Lord?"

"For I sought the Lord and He delivered me of all my fears." Ps. 34:4 KJV

Chapter Twenty-Six

Jim's Deliverance

Back in 1979, I was going to a church called The Lord's Chapel. One day as I walked into the church through a side entrance, I looked over to the right where there was a stairwell. Underneath the dark stairwell was a guy I knew, crouched in sort of a fetal position. I had always thought of him as a rational man. He was a young man in his thirties.

I said, "Jim? Is that you?"

He didn't answer me. I went under the stairwell a bit more and said, "Jim? What are you doing in here?"

"I've got a demon."

"You've got a demon? Jim, are you joking with me?"

He answered, "Go get Brother Parsons!"

"Why do you want him?"

"He can help me."

"Jim, come on man, are you kidding me?"

"No." He was speaking in a gruff voice I had never heard him speak in before, as if he was scared. I didn't want to leave him because I thought he was mentally ill at the time.

So, I called to somebody else entering the church and said, "Go get Brother Parsons and his wife. Tell them it's an emergency and to please come to this place right now." They left to go get them.

I went back to speak to Jim. I said, "Jim, what do you mean, a demon? What are you talking about? What would you call it, does it have a name?"

He said, "Homosexuality."

"Homosexuality? Alright." I didn't know what to say then because it kind of freaked me out.

I waited with Jim until Brother Parsons and his wife came. They were a young couple, probably in their thirties. I was in my late twenties. I told Brother Parsons, "Brother Jim says he has a demon. He says he needs you." Then I let him take over.

Brother Parsons said, "Jim, what is the problem?"

"I've got a demon."

"What do you mean, a demon?"

Jim said, "Homosexuality."

"Jim, do you want to be set free?"

"Yeah, that's why I asked for you."

Brother Parsons spoke to his wife and they both agreed to try to help Jim. They indicated that we needed to go to a more private room.
Brother Parsons said, "John, do you want to come along?"
"Well, I don't know."

"If you'd like to, you're welcome to come along."

I told my wife to go on into the church and I would go with Brother Parsons and his wife. The four of us went to the private room. Chairs circled the outside of the room. Brother

Parsons pulled two chairs together and he and Jim sat knee-to-knee. His wife took a chair on the side, so I took my cue from her and sat over on the side. I didn't know what to do. I was just a new, young Christian, and I had eyes wide open. So, I would say things to myself like "In the name of Jesus. Lord, please help here. I plead the Blood of Jesus." I don't remember exactly what I said, but I remember saying the name of Jesus.

I did see something that day. As I've said sometimes, I saw a thing. What I saw was not with my eyes, but I definitely saw it with my soul and with my understanding and with my spirit. What I saw was an anointing on Brother Parsons. It was in the way he spoke to Jim like he really cared. I can't describe it but what I saw was compassion. When he spoke to Jim, he would ask him a question, and it was in a soft (yet not fake) voice, as if he was really listening and really cared.

He said, "Jim, do you want to be set free?"

"YES! "

Brother Parsons began to lead us in prayer. He asked the Father, in the name of Jesus, for authority over the demonic world that was in Jim. He said something like, "Jim, we plead the blood of Jesus over you. In the name of Jesus, we cast out this demon." Then he looked at Jim and said, "Do you feel relief? Do you feel peace?"

Jim growled, in a gruff voice, "No!"

"Well, let me ask you this, Jim. That big, old thick gold chain around your neck—did your lover give you that chain?"

Jim shook his head, "Yes."

"Jim, take that chain off." All of a sudden there seemed to be an new intensity in Brother Parsons. He sat up on the edge of his chair and commanded, "Now, you foul spirit, name yourself!"

A voice came out of Jim that sounded really weird. I was thinking that this guy was a good actor, or this was the strangest thing I've ever heard. The voice said, "Hyglogaloid."

Brother Parsons said, "You foul spirit, Hyglogaloid, I cast you out from Jim. You've got to leave him NOW in Jesus' name." Jim just looked the same. He said, "Jim, let me ask you this. Do you have peace now, do you feel release?"

"Nooo!"

Brother Parsons once again got that intensity. He said, "Now, you second foul spirit, you name yourself."

All of a sudden Jim's face changed, and his voice changed. It sounded just as crazily intense, but it was a different sounding voice. An octave higher, He said, "Eclepsod!" or some sort of strange name that I had never heard.

Brother Parsons said, "Eclepsod, I cast you out in Jesus' name!" All of a sudden Jim let out a huge sigh of relief. His arms slunk to his side and his whole face looked different.

Brother Parsons said, "Now Jim, do you feel release?"

"Yes, yes, I feel release!"

"Jim, stand up. We're going to ask for the Spirit of God to fill you now." When he laid his hands on his forehead and began to pray, all of a sudden it was like a fire hose got stuck in Jim's belly and he began to speak in tongues like I had never heard anyone speak in tongues. I can't even begin to describe how loudly it was coming out of his mouth.

Brother Parsons said, "He's set free, John. He's set free. Jim, do you want to go to church?"

Jim didn't answer. His head was still up towards

heaven, and tongues were pouring out of his mouth. He continued to speak in tongues as we walked across the parking lot and even as he took a seat in the back of the sanctuary. I went to take my seat with Debbie.

That was the last I saw of Jim, because we left to go to Pensacola, Florida. I had to move because of my job and because the Lord had told me to go. A year later we came back for a reunion. I was walking toward that same back side door, and I saw a guy walking across the parking lot.
I said, "Jim! Is that you?"

"John!"

I said, "How are you doing, man?"

"Free ever since!"

"These signs will accompany those who have believed: in My name they will cast out demons, they will speak in new tongues." Mark 16:17 NASB

Yes, that was the day of Jim's Deliverance. As for me, it was just an ordinary man's experience with God.

Chapter Twenty-Seven

The Lord Wakes Buck Up

This story is about one of my favorite people in all the world. His name is Buck Waters, William B. Waters or Dr. Waters. I first met Dr. Waters in 1980 when I went to work for my brother-in-law, Dr. Herschel Stanford. Hershel was, at that time, a chiropractor in Pensacola, FL and Buck was his associate. We were both new at Stanford Chiropractic. I think Buck had been working for six months when I started.

Buck was (is) just a great guy. He was very helpful to me and very kind; he wanted to teach me what he knew about chiropractic and about x-ray. He taught me skillfully about x-ray so that when I took my x-ray test, I passed easily.

I was at that time in my life when I knew the Lord had led me to Pensacola. I would call myself an on-fire Christian, which means different things to different people. To some people that's good; some people would say they didn't like that because they didn't want somebody who was always bubbling over about the Lord.

I wasn't trying to beat people over the head with the Bible, but I decided that I was a disciple. A loyal, loving learner of Jesus Christ. I decided that I wanted to be a witness of the Lord's goodness and the Lord's mercy, and the Lord's joy. I wanted to be a witness in every scene. Sometimes people don't understand what I mean by that. Life is hard to figure. It seems to me like it's one scene that changes after another. It might be that you're riding in the car, riding along by yourself. Well, in that scene I want to remember the Lord, so I'll praise Him, or maybe pray and talk to the Lord. Or maybe you're with somebody. I'll go home and be with my wife, and I want to be a witness for the Lord by listening to her. Or it might be that you're going into work or you're taking x-rays of somebody. Every time I want to bring the subject around to the goodness of the Lord, somehow tell of the goodness of the Lord.

I was a new Christian, and I would try to witness to everybody. Somehow Buck was responsive. He had been in the Catholic faith and had a little bit of fear of the Lord but hadn't really been going to church. He was an interesting guy to me. He loved sports and had been a basketball player. He was a really good surfer and loved to surf.
Buck just had a cheerful personality. He could turn what seemed like a lemon into lemonade. He could make you laugh in the midst of something that looked like it was a serious matter. It wasn't like he was trying to be a jokester, but he was just really positive.

Well, I liked this guy Buck. He just drew the witness of the Lord out of me. There was another associate at the time, and he didn't seem to like it. He didn't like the fact that I would write a scripture every day and put it on the podium, or that I would be whistling or singing as I walked through the clinic. Sometimes I would pray with patients. I prayed with one of the other doctor's patients, and the patient said they got healed and didn't want chiropractic care. This doctor was just furious that I had prayed with his patient. I can understand that, it was his patient.

He wanted me fired. He went to my brother-in-law and said that praying for his patients wasn't right, and he wanted me fired. Thank God I had favor with my brother-in-law, and my brother-in-law felt that because of the presence of the Lord, we were being blessed. So, he told that particular doctor that this clinic was a Christian clinic and that he encouraged prayer.

It wasn't that way with Buck. Buck and I got along so well. This story is called "The Lord Wakes Up Buck."

This story begins when Buck and I were going to take a trip to a conference on chiropractic. On this particular trip, Dr. Stanford and his wife went in another vehicle. They had a van that Buck and I were going to drive and take three of the CA's (chiropractic assistants that happened to be ladies) and ride to Atlanta.

We worked until five o'clock, which meant that by us taking the van at that time of night, it took about five hours to get to Atlanta. We were going to get there late that night. I was driving and Buck was sitting up front, as we were heading to Atlanta. I was drinking coffee, and I was excited to share about the Lord. I just shared the gospel, and I shared it from A to Z, and from Genesis to Revelation. I gave my testimony and what I knew about the goodness of the Lord. I was so excited and talking fast, and it seemed that Buck was listening to every word. Actually, the girls in the back were listening to every word. I was high on caffeine and the Holy Ghost.

We got into Atlanta at about midnight. We knew we had

to get up the next morning, and we were so tired. We knew it was late, and we said, "What time do you think we should get up?" We said that since it was so late, we would make it eight o'clock. That's what we agreed on.

Buck and I were staying in the same room. We got to thinking, eight o'clock isn't early enough. We needed to get up earlier than that. We needed to get up at seven. I said, "Do you think we should get a wake-up call?"

Buck said, "Well, we could ask the Lord to wake us up."

I thought that was so cool because it was faith that Buck would ask the Lord to wake us up. So, we prayed right there. I said, "Jesus, would you wake us up at seven o'clock sharp?" Buck and I smiled and said, "Amen." We believed He would.

We told the girls to call us at eight o'clock. Well, I was so high on caffeine and the Holy Ghost that I couldn't even go to sleep. I decided to write my brother-in-law, Butch, a letter about my testimony and the plan of salvation. At that time Butch wasn't going to church. It was difficult for me to write; it takes me a while to write, even a small card. But I began to write this letter. I wrote and I wrote, and I don't know what time I got finished, but it was several pages. It seemed like it was even longer than that. I think it was around three in the morning when I went to bed. I was very tired by that time, so I just conked out into a deep sleep.

Next news you know, I was in the midst of a dream. In this dream I saw Satan, and he was huge. He was maybe ten times as big as me. He looked like he was taller than the tallest pine tree. He was very big, and I was small, way small. In that dream I didn't even come up halfway to his ankle. I was very small. It seemed like he was overpowering me. So, I called out to Jesus. About that time, Jesus steps into this scene in my dream, and He does something that I never necessarily thought Jesus would do. He took His right forearm and made a move with it that I had known to be a strong move of a football player blocking. It's a lifting of the forearm, and kind of a strike with the forearm. With His right forearm, He moved it forward and basically hit Satan and moved him out of the way. I had seen this move done by my dad; my dad had powerful arms. It was a powerful right forearm. I had seen that move, so when Jesus hit Satan with that right forearm and bumped him out of the way, at that exact second our phone rang in our room.

I sat up and said, "Buck, what time do you think it is?"

He had this big smile and he said, "It's gotta be seven."

It was exactly seven o'clock. When I bolted up out of that bed and I looked, it was straight up seven o'clock. It was the girls next door, the CAs. They had decided that instead of calling us at eight they would call us at seven.

So that dream meant a lot to Buck and his young faith. It meant a lot to me. It was like a miracle, the fact that it was not just my mental alarm clock. There was a dream about Jesus, and when He moved Satan out of the way, then the phone rang. Not only that, it was the girls. There was something about that, that raises the question; is God really the God of circumstances, of life like that? It meant a lot to Buck.

I continued to witness to Buck at work, and we enjoyed it. Then one day I heard that a musical band named the Songwriters was coming to Pensacola. I had heard them up in Tennessee when I belonged to a church called the Lord's Chapel. The Songwriters had played there many times.

They were a unique and cool Christian band. They had long hair and long beards and, in the past, had played in bars. The Songwriters were great musicians. Their wonderful testimony was so real and genuine, and when they would do their concert, the whole concert was around salvation. Yeah, they would play their songs—they had a bunch of funny songs, all that they had written—but towards the end it would get more serious about the Lord and salvation. I knew that somebody would get saved at their concert every time, sometimes quite a few people.

So, I said, "Buck, the Songwriters are coming to Pensacola. Will you go with me?"

He said, "Oh yeah, I'll go with you."

So Debbie, Buck and I went to hear the Songwriters at a church on the other side of town. It was called Grace Assembly. We went, and the concert was good. They did their concert and we enjoyed it so much, but then when they began to get serious about the gospel, the Spirit of the Lord came upon Buck and he got drunk in the Spirit. Some of you won't understand what that means and some of you laugh and say, "I know what it means."

The Spirit came on Buck so strong, and when these guys had an altar call, to come to Jesus, Buck knocked over two chairs, fell and crawled to the altar to receive the Lord. He just had a tremendous salvation experience that night. Buck then joined that church and was with them, and then at Olive Baptist Church for twenty years. He has also started a church called The Upper Room in Gulf Breeze Florida. It is going very strong. He also travels around the world to Christian Surfers meetings and speaks.

That was the story about the time that the "Lord Woke Buck Up." And now I'm talking to you. Time to wake up, my friend! "Awake, O sleeper, rise up from the dead, and Christ will give you light."

Ephesians 5:14 NLT

Chapter Twenty-Eight

"Lost in Twelve-Foot Seas, but Great Peace"

This story starts out on a winter day in the early 80's. Dr. Hershel Stanford, another friend named Herb, and I wanted to go fishing in a boat that Dr. Stanford owned.

The weather was really bad. We definitely couldn't go out into the Gulf because of a small craft warning. The boat was a twenty-five-foot Grady White, made for rough seas. I thought, "Well, this is a good boat. What we'll do is go ride in the sound, which is fairly safe. I'm always up for a good adventure." I guess you don't get adventures, my friends, unless you take a little risk. On this winter day, it was cold, but the boat had a good windshield and a cabin. So, we went out in the sound, and the wind was blowing pretty hard. We rode to the Pensacola Pass, where the sound meets the Gulf of Mexico. The waves were way too big in the pass; they were about 10 feet high.

Herschel said, "Ah, come on John! Outside the pass, the waves will surely calm down to probably about 8 foot. You know how it was, we fished one other time in 8 footers all day…come on, John."

I said, "Herschel, there's a small craft warning, and there's a good chance a wave could capsize our boat out there."

He said, "Come on John, I'm willing to do it." You see, Herschel, the family called him "Pete," is a bit of an adrenaline junky. He used to race cars and motorcycles. In some races they would jump motorcycles. Jump them? To me that's a little bit crazy. I mean the thrill of the jump is not worth the agony of the broken bones. There is a balance needed between love of the thrill and wise caution. If I feel I'm in control, I like a little risk in life. I call life my venturous adventure.

I have this saying that I do live by, at least I lived by it that particular day, and some people would say it's a foolish statement. Great-grandchild, I'm not saying for you to live by this statement, but this is what your great granddaddy lived by. I heard an Indian say it on a movie one time, that's where I picked it up. Here it is: "It's a good day to die." I figure, as a Christian, it is a good day to die. Paul, an apostle and a light to the Gentiles in the Bible, said "To die is gain." He said, "In the presence of the Lord is fullness of joy," and "To be absent from the body is to be present with the Lord." So, everybody says they want to see Jesus—I say why not today? So, I live like it's a good day to die.

I told Herschel, "Herschel, it's really foolish, but you know my saying, 'It's a good day to die.'"

So we foolishly headed out through the pass. As we went out, instead of the waves getting smaller, about three-quarters of the way out of the pass, they greatly increased to what I estimated to be twelve feet high, with crashing, rolling waves. It was like a man could surf each wave. I had never seen them like that.

Now you would be saying, "Great-granddad, you're just an exaggerator." But no, grandson or granddaughter, I'm not exaggerating, because I know waves. I'm talking about from the belly or the bottom of that wave to the crest, it was twelve feet high.

So, whenever you're taking a wave like that, you have to quarter it, which means that instead of going straight into it, you go on a forty-five degree angle so that when you go over the wave, you can ride down the other side. Sometimes, even when we quartered a wave and came over the top, it would seem like I could count to six or seven before the boat would hit the bottom again. That means we're falling that far. When we'd hit the bottom, it felt like the entire boat was going to crack in half—it would go BAM, a big loud bam.

By this time, Herb, who I would say was an intellectual man, a wonderful man, was more than a little afraid and rightly so. He was wisely pleading for me to turn the boat around. Herschel was not a merciful man, and I think he kind of enjoyed Herb being so uncomfortable.

Herschel's hair was disheveled, and he had a crazy grin on his face. Herb's hair was also a mess and his face was pale white with a far off look on his face. I felt for him and wanted to turn the boat around.

But Herschel kept saying, "If we can just get a little way outside the pass, maybe they'll settle back down to 8 footers."

I thought maybe the waves would decrease. When the water is on an incoming tide and the wind is blowing out through the pass toward the south as it was, it will build the waves just in the pass. When you make it out through the pass sometimes the size of the waves decrease. I have to admit this experience was thrilling. I was grinning also.

We kept hitting those waves, hitting those waves. After we had been going for half an hour, we had only made it perhaps three miles out of the pass.

I told Herschel, "This is ridiculous. This isn't even fun. I'm going to turn the boat around, we are heading back."

What I chose to do was get behind one of those big waves, because they were heading in towards the pass. We stayed right behind a giant wave. Then we looked behind us, and it took our breath away. There was a twelve-footer that looked like a mountain of white water was going to come crashing right into the back of the boat.

So, as we're riding there, Herschel, I'm sorry for saying this, had absolutely no sense. He said, "John, couldn't we just fish a little? Couldn't we throw out a spoon and maybe we'd catch a bonito or something like that?" I couldn't believe he said that.

I said, "Herschel, the poles are down underneath in the cabin!" But then I said, "Ok, I'll go down and get my life preserver. Here, Herschel take the wheel."

We had many life preservers. I had put one on each of them, but I didn't have one on. I went down into the cabin and got a life preserver. I came back up and set my life preserver down instead of putting it on. I took a pole and flipped it out the back.

All of a sudden, Herschel said, "Watch this" and he took the boat over the top of one of the waves, and then raced down the bottom like he was surfing. He made a little noise that sounded like "Weeeee!!" as we were going down that wave. Then he sped the boat up to about 20 knots and went up over the top of another one.

I said, "Herschel, no, nooooo!! If you do that, you're going to sink us!!"

About that time, he raced down the second wave and the bow went under the wave in front of us, and the big wave behind us crashed up and sprung me like I was on a springboard, right out of the side of the boat. I hit that cold water and I looked up and saw Herb's face. He was leaning out of the back of the boat reaching in vain for me. I promise you, it looked like his face had grown one inch longer in a stretch of agony. He looked at me and went, "Ohhhhhh......"

Herschel did have enough sense that he said, "Herb, don't take your eyes off him!" He knew if he got very far from me, I'd be lost in the valleys of the waves, and they might not be able to see me again.

Herschel did a quick spin move, even though it was dangerous, and almost turned the boat over sideways on the big wave, and began to head up the next wave.

Great-grandchild, when I hit the water, because I'm a Christian, I had great PEACE. I know some may not understand that, but instead of my heart racing, I had great peace. I spoke out into the environment, and this is what I advise you to do. In the midst of your situation, you call on the Lord. You call Him and speak to Him. It would probably be best if you could remember a Scripture, but this is what I said at that time. I know it might seem a little corny, but this is what I said.

"So God, this is your bathtub."

As I said that, I just kind of chuckled. It seemed like He was holding me up or something. I'm not that great a swimmer, but it seemed like I was just there floating high in the water.

I saw Herschel go up another big wave, and then he put the engines in reverse. Then, I did have a slight fear, because I thought I was going to get churned up in one of those twin outboard props. The back of the boat with those spinning propellers were racing backwards right toward me. I thought, "I've got to duck-dive." But I had on tennis shoes, a jacket and jeans, and sometimes it's not easy to dive. But right before I got ready to dive, Herb threw a rope.

Herb didn't have what I would call a good roper's mentality about how far he could throw a rope; he threw it way too soon and the rope was way too short. But he threw it anyway, and it went right back and got wrapped in the port prop shutting down that engine.

When I saw that, I thought, "Yesssss! Praise the Lord." I knew right then that I could swim to that engine because it was off. So immediately I swam, and the boat came back to me. I swam until I got there. I went straight to that engine, climbed up on that engine, and, all of a sudden, I did have a strong authority come over me. I knew that no longer was Herschel even slightly the captain of that boat.
I said, "Herschel, raise up that port engine." I jumped back there and got the rope unwrapped, and said, "Now get out of the way."

Then I took the wheel. I followed one of those big waves all the way in. In the meantime, they gave me a dry jacket and life preserver. They dried me off a little, but I was not letting any man have that wheel.

After all was said and done, we got back to the house. I took a good hot shower, and Debbie was taking good care of me like always, fixing me some hot soup and coffee. I sat in my big old Lazy Boy chair in my living room, and when I got up to go in the kitchen, my legs collapsed from underneath me. I fell straight to the living room floor. I think that was aftershock. My adrenaline had raced so high and then depleted. But I thought it was a neat experience, because I had never had my legs go out from under me.

Here's what I want to say to you, great-grandchild or whoever else is reading this story: no matter what the situation--huge waves, fire, peril--you can call on the name of the Lord and know Him. My question is: do you know Him? If you're in an airplane that is about to crash and you know you're going to die, are you going to praise Him? Or are you going to scream and freak out? I believe that what I'm going to do is say, "Hey Lord, here I come!" And praise Him, because I know Him and I have great peace. We all die, count on it! You can have peace. Call to the Lord. Get to know Him.

The proof is in the pudding. I knew Him the day I was "Lost In Twelve-Foot Seas, But Great Peace "

Chapter Twenty-Nine

Song of Deliverance

Back in 1982, we had moved to Pensacola from Tennessee. We were going to a church called Liberty Northeast. I was a fairly young Christian and trying to follow the Lord with all my heart.

I had begun to minister at the Pensacola City Jail on Sunday nights. I would go every Sunday night at six o'clock with a brother from the church named Tim. Tim loved to share the Word; he just had an open, real faith. I, on the other hand, was a very timid Christian. I wanted to share my faith, but I found it difficult at times, especially in jail. I would let Tim do all the talking; it was like I was hiding behind his apron, so to speak, like a little boy. He would speak and I would listen, or maybe I would share a little bit.

That was going along fine until one day a Methodist jail chaplain took charge. He didn't know what to make of us charismatic boys, those of us that loved the Spirit, the inner workings of the Spirit, and the gifts of the Spirit. It seemed like he gave us a little bit of a hard time.

So, on this one night when this brother was in charge, for some reason he wanted to separate Tim and me. Perhaps it was the Lord. Sometimes when you have to go through a change or be something different, you'll grow.

This night he separated the ministers and made us go by ourselves. So, I was led by a guard back to a particular group of cells by myself. To be honest, it was kinda scary, but of course, I never let on.

You go back through a number of different gates or cell doors, and they really clang when they shut. The guard led me to a group of prisoners that were all in the same cell block, so to speak. It was like you were up above them looking down into where they lived. They were somewhat free to move around at that time in their cell block. There were no windows. It was like we were in the bowels of the prison.

There might have been a dozen prisoners in this cell block. Some of them were showering, some of them were watching TV, and some of them were playing cards. There were some tables they could sit at. At the gate to the cell block there was a cubicle of cell bars that was probably about 8 x 8, and they shut the gate behind me, so I was in a cage, 8 x 8, looking through the bars at prisoners.

They could come up and stand in front of those bars if they chose to. Things have greatly changed at the jail now; you can only speak to them behind wire or glass. You can't give them anything or take anything in. Of course, I wasn't trying to give them anything but the Gospel. I was there to share the Word of truth with them.

On this night I was standing there, by myself, and these guys were all doing their activities. I did not know WHAT to say. I didn't know how to start. They saw me; I saw them. They were kind of ignoring me, and finally I said in a timid voice, "Does anybody want to share the Word of the Lord? Does anybody want to talk about the Lord or talk about the Bible?"

There were three guys sitting at a table that was close to me. One of them looked so mean. He had long scraggly unwashed hair and sort of a scraggly beard, with a frown on his forehead. He didn't have a shirt on. He stared at me and growled. I could tell that he was intimidating the two guys he was with, and he was intimidating me.

So, what do you do? I felt like Moses. Moses said one time in the Bible, "God, I don't know what to say. I don't have eloquent words. I don't have the knowledge. I don't know what to do." But here's what I want to tell you. Just like God told Moses, if you'll begin to speak by faith, and only listen and hear by the Spirit, He'll put the words in your mouth. Jesus said that. He said, "I'll give you the words to speak. In that hour, I'll give you the words."

I didn't know what to do. So, I prayed silently, "Help me, Lord Jesus. What do I do? What do I say?" I heard the Holy Spirit say, "Sing in the Spirit to them."

I looked at that mean-looking guy glaring up at me and I began to do something by faith that I've never, ever done before. I began to sing in the Spirit. Some of you won't know what that means, but for us in our charismatic way, we believe in the baptism of the Holy Spirit with evidence of speaking in tongues. Singing in the Spirit is singing in tongues. Others will say that tongues are for your private prayer closet, and a prayer unto God. I'm not sure where all that fits doctrinally, but I needed the Holy Spirit at that moment and that's what I heard Him say to do.

So, I stared at that big mean guy, eyeball to eyeball,

and I began to sing in the Spirit. I began to sing gently, not loudly, but loud enough that everybody in the cell block could hear me. As I looked at him, he just looked like he got all frustrated and he growled again and walked off toward the back. When he went off to the back, I quit singing in tongues and I said boldly, "Hey, you two guys want to talk about the Gospel?"

They both came up. One had never received Christ before; the other was a backslider. So, as we shared the plan of salvation and shared the Lord, the one guy came back to the Lord and the other guy made a profession of faith. By faith, I believe they're saved today.

So, I say, don't have fear. Look to the Lord, see if you can hear Him. Make a step of faith and He'll show up.

He did that night, with a... Song of Deliverance.

"You are my hiding place. You will preserve me from trouble. You will surround me with songs of deliverance." Psalms 32:7

Chapter Thirty

The Miracle

What is a miracle? I've heard it said that a miracle is an unexplained happening, that the only explanation has to be that God performed it. Sometimes I think people call things miracles that are not. They use the word pretty lightly.

One day I believe I saw a miracle. This miracle happened to me, when I was on my way to work. I used to walk to work, and I would cut through some woods. I would go in fairly early and get to work at about 7:30 A.M. I would leave my house early because my custom was to stop at an oak tree about halfway through the woods. I'd usually sit down on the roots of this oak tree on a notebook, and I would read my Bible and pray. Some days I would have to fight the mosquitoes as I would sit trying to read my Bible.

On this particular day, I turned to a passage in Revelation that says, "To him that overcomes I will give a white robe of righteousness." I read that verse and was meditating on it. I knew that to have that white robe of righteousness meant you were accepted in the Lord. There's another place in the Bible that says, "Accepted in the beloved."

At the time that this happened, I was a Christian. If you had asked me if I was a Christian, I would have said, "Yes, I'm a Christian." But in my private thought life, at times I had doubts.

Please allow me to digress, to give some understanding to these doubts. The Lord had dealt with me for what seemed like all my life. I had an experience with the Lord when I was five years old, then again when I was at camp when I was thirteen, then at nineteen at the University of Georgia. In 1969, as a lonely freshman, my Forestry professor led me in the sinner's prayer and I began to go to a Baptist church. Was I really saved? I sure thought so.

However later that year, 69', I had a major backslide. I couldn't tell my family or my girlfriend, who is now my wife, what had happened to me. I was afraid they wouldn't understand. I stopped going to church and started hanging out again with my college drinking buddies. I went strongly into the ways of the world with drinking and some drugs and was basically raising hell again.

It wasn't until ten years later that I became broken and called out to the Lord. He heard my cry and saved me. My wife and my son and I were all baptized the same Sunday morning. I was really saved, sanctified and filled with the Holy Ghost. I have never looked back. However, at times I battled doubts in my mind. Now, fast forward to the day of the miracle.

Even though this was years later and I had been saved and in the church for maybe five or six years and was even ministering at the jail, at times I would have this doubt: was I really saved? After all, in the past, I had that major back slide and I did so many bad things. Was I really saved? Could and did He really forgive me? There is a place in the Bible that talks about these virgins, those that were so clean and had never sinned. I knew I had greatly sinned, so I would have these doubts.

By faith, I believed Jesus died for my sins. His precious blood paid a ransom for me. A price I could never pay. He delivered me from the kingdom of darkness and placed me in His marvelous kingdom of light. I believed He rose from the grave and ever lives at the right hand of God. I believed these things. I studied the Word and went to church regularly. I know I was and am saved. But at times I would battle doubts. I cried for deliverance and the Lord heard me and helped me. And this is the story of an ordinary man's experience with God. Actually, I believe the Lord did this thing for me that really helped me believe and rest in His acceptance and forgiveness. There are many things that encourage you as you walk your walk with the Lord, but this was one specific thing He did for me.

The Miracle:

I believe that sometimes a miracle is meant for just one person and not for another; because Jesus did miracles and many still didn't believe in Him. Yet for the one who received the miracle, it changed their life.

And now for the miracle. On this day as I sat under the oak tree, as was my custom, I began reading the Bible. I read about a robe of righteousness that is promised. The Word says, "The one overcoming thus will be clothed in white garments. And I will never blot out his name from the book of life, and I will confess his name before My Father and before His angels."

I was looking up into the blue sky and I said, "Father, I

want to know, I want to KNOW if I'm forgiven. I want to know if I'll have this robe of righteousness. I want this garment."

As I looked up into the sky, I saw a flicker, just a tiny flicker that looked like a leaf that helicoptered in the sky by spinning around and around. But it wasn't a leaf. Here it came down out of the sky, and it was helicoptering and spinning. It was three inches long and a quarter inch wide, and it was a piece of paper spinning. It spun right down to my feet, and I picked it up. In all bold, capital letters it said, "THIS GARMENT PASSES INSPECTION."

Now, I ask you, where did that come from? Did it come out of somebody's coat and then was swept up into the air? Or maybe out of an airplane? I don't know. Since then, I have seen a few things in pockets and in clothes that said, "This garment inspected by No. 63", but I've never seen one that says "THIS GARMENT PASSES INSPECTION" just like that.

The Lord did a miracle for me that day. To me, it meant that I'm accepted into the beloved, and that I'm going to have a white robe of righteousness. It's not because of something I've earned. You see, as it says in Isaiah, "My righteousness is as filthy rags." But when we put on Christ, we put on His righteousness because we become justified by what His sacrifice did for man, what it did for me. So, as I put my faith in Jesus, I am qualified for this garment. It's a robe of righteousness that passes inspection.

So I ask you—was this a miracle? It was to this ordinary man telling a story of his experiences with God.

Chapter Thirty-One

The Lord Heals Isaac's Big Toe

When my son Isaac was a little boy, he had an unusual custom for a lad. He liked to dress himself. Every day he would pull all his clothes out of his tall dresser drawer and try them on all different ways. When he was finished there would be a big pile of clothes on the floor. This was when he was probably about three years old, maybe four. Every day was the same ritual—he would pull all his clothes out and try them on.

One day he was trying to pull some clothes out of the upper drawers. It was a big old chest of drawers made of solid oak. He was climbing up those drawers and pulled back on one of the top drawers, and the whole big chest of drawers (it weighed a lot) fell over, came down, and landed right on his big toe. He began to scream! I came racing in there and picked the dresser up off him, and his big toe was split, and it was spurting out blood. He screamed like no child I've ever heard scream. So, I immediately wrapped a cloth around it and carried him to his mother. She held him in a rocking chair in the living room.

Well, the week before I had heard a story in church about a little kid who, during the Sunday morning service in the nursery, a little boy cut himself and pierced an artery. They brought the child in to the service and the pastor went straight to the scripture. It was a scripture in Mark 16:17. It says, "These signs shall follow those that believe: they shall lay hands on the sick and they shall recover..."This pastor read that scripture out loud before he prayed, and that little kid was healed. He said that what we need to do at times is read that scripture out loud and believe God's promise and declare it in a faith-based prayer.

Remembering that admonition, with my son Isaac still screaming, I went immediately to the Bible and I read that scripture out loud. I read, "These signs shall follow those that believe." I read it out loud to Isaac and Debbie and then I laid hands on him. He was screaming loudly and when I prayed, suddenly, like a miracle, Isaac just conked out, like he went unconscious. He fell right asleep on Debbie's chest. He went from screaming to totally asleep. I was so afraid that if I picked him up and carried him, he would start screaming, but I picked him up and carried him to his bed. He laid there and slept for a couple hours.

When he got up, he ran around on that foot and never even acted like it hurt. There was no bleeding. The toe was split through the nail, but he never cried about it again. To me, that was a miracle.

That was the day "The Lord Healed Isaac's Big Toe."

"Therefore I say unto you, What things so ever ye desire, when ye pray, believe that ye receive them, and ye shall have them." Jesus The Lord Mark 11:24 KJV

Chapter Thirty-Two

Do You Believe I Know God?

Alright great-grandson or great-granddaughter, this is your Papa John, telling you a story of what happened to me at sea one day. I think this story is somewhat of an example of how a person can hear God.

I'm not sure how old you are, but you may have heard about a concept called a "premonition." If you understand what a premonition is, it seems like it's a warning about something to come. It's usually foreboding and somehow a person instinctively knows that something is going to happen in the future that might not be good.

I believe in God. I believe He can speak to us. I believe He does speak to us. For one thing, in His Word, He says that He speaks to us, and that if we will open our ears and listen, we can hear Him and He can instruct or warn us. Jesus said, "My sheep know My voice." One place in the Bible the Holy Spirit says, "Let peace rule in your heart like an umpire." So sometimes, if you're trying to make a decision, you can look to see if you have peace about it. If you know the Lord, you call it the peace of God.

On this day, I was with "Uncle Herschel." Uncle Herschel Stanford was married to my sister, Jane Newlin Stanford. Herschel and I worked together. I helped him purchase a boat, a used twenty-foot Robalo with a new 200 Evinrude motor on it.

We were so excited. We were going to fish in a billfishing tournament—billfishing meaning fishing for white marlin or blue marlin. We got into a tournament, which cost us $350 each. We had some big new expensive rods and reels, and everything was decked out. Herschel had a couple thousand dollars just in this tournament. We looked at the weather forecast, which said it was bright and sunny, with low winds and very smooth. With this particular boat, you wouldn't want to go too far offshore if it was high seas. That beautiful morning the seas were just about flat and everything looked very good.

So, we headed out to go about 30 miles into the Gulf of Mexico. When we had gone approximately 15 miles out into the Gulf, and like I said, the water was perfectly blue with beautiful sunshine, and it was about 7 o'clock in the morning. All of a sudden, I felt so terrible down deep inside. My first thought was, am I seasick? But I really don't get seasick, and I had never gotten seasick on a beautiful day, never ever. So here it was, a beautiful day, and I felt terribly sick, but it wasn't in my stomach. It was somewhere in the center of me. I stopped in my mind and I said, "God, are You speaking to me?"

What I heard was, "Head for the shore!"

I told Herschel, "Pull back on the throttle. Stop the boat. I believe I just heard from the Lord that we're supposed to head for the shore."

He said, "What?? It's beautiful! I spent all this money! We can't go to the shore! John, what is the problem? We can't go to the shore; we're already 15 miles out. We can't do that!"

I grabbed Herschel with both hands by the collar and pulled us nose to nose and said to him, "Herschel, do you believe that I know God?" I was looking him in the eye.

He said, "John, I don't understand why we should possibly go back, but, yes, I know that you know God!"

We turned our boat around and headed for shore as fast as we could. When we got into the pass, we were taking on so much water in the back of the boat that our portable gas tanks were floating in the back of the boat. The water got up to knee deep and we were so close to sinking. I was finally able to get the plug out to drain it enough to get to the marina, but we almost sank. If we had gone on further out in the gulf, we would have surely sunk or capsized in the Gulf of Mexico.

So, you would say, "What happened, Papa John? How did you know?"

Well, I'm telling you, it was a sense that I had deep inside, where I didn't have peace. That's all I can tell you. Then, when I prayed, I felt like I heard, not audibly, but I heard by what I believe was God's Spirit to my spirit, and from my spirit to my soul. Your soul is your mind, your will and your emotions, and I interpreted it as: "HEAD TO THE SHORE."

Here's what I say to you—I believe that God does speak, and on that day He saved our lives, or at least saved us from a major hassle of going down at sea. Do you believe you know God?

Chapter Thirty-Three

Isaac Loves Justice

The old Ike-Man. Isaac Taylor Thomas Newlin. He's my second son. He was born in 1983 in Pensacola, FL. Isaac has always been a very special young man.

Even from an early age it seemed that he had unusual common sense. This would show up in different ways. You could ask him when he was eight years old, "Isaac, what do you think? What temperament do you think that person has?" And he would say, "They're a melancholic phlegmatic." He had heard us talking about temperaments, and he learned to identify them in someone very quickly.

Another way I could tell that Isaac was special was other people's positive impression of him. My dad was an excellent judge of character. It was said of my Dad or at least I said it of him, that he could weigh a man's salt by just looking at him. What that means is my dad could tell if a guy had what it takes to be a man according to my dad's standard, and he had a very high standard. To give an example, if we were going someplace without my dad, he would ask us, "Is Isaac going?" And we would say yes, and my dad would say "You'll be all right then". My dad would often say that Isaac had a keen sense of judgment.

When Isaac was a young boy, I would read a chapter of the book of Proverbs in the Bible to him every night. I would stop after each verse and ask him what it meant. At first, he couldn't tell me and I would explain it. It wasn't long until he could tell me every time just what it meant. I believe Isaac gained Wisdom from the Word of God, "the God of all wisdom."

I would see this love of justice when Isaac would play with his friends and how he would react to what was fair and what was right. He just has an extraordinary dose of common sense and wisdom. Some people say that common sense isn't common. It seems like not everybody's got it, but Isaac sure did and still does.

I believe that I marked Isaac as a young man. I marked him in this way: I said a statement over him, and I repeated it over and over again. I said, "Isaac loves justice". I said it many times, "Isaac loves justice." It marked him and it stuck because it was so true. I knew it was the Lord. It was like I heard the Lord say it over Isaac.

His mother called him a bulldog. When he believed he was right on a subject, he would not turn loose or relent. One example of this occurred at school.

Isaac went to a Christian elementary school where his teacher was a Baptist. This teacher said in class that speaking in tongues was not for this dispensation, that it went away, and it was just for the time of the early disciples. But Isaac said, "No, it's for today." And the teacher said, "Well, do you speak in tongues?" and Isaac said, "No, but I can prove by the scriptures that speaking in tongues is for today!"

So, they set up a time and a place for a debate about this subject. At the end of the debate, the teacher said, "Well, Isaac, I have to say that you've done such a good job that you win." And what I saw there was that when Isaac had made up his mind regarding a subject or a concept or something that he believed to be true, he was willing to defend it or contend for the faith, as the Bible would say. Not in a way that would be argumentative or rebellious or even stubborn, but he had the tenacity and perseverance when he believed in something. Yes, Debbie, he is like a bulldog.

The story of "Isaac Loves Justice" was confirmed at an early age when Isaac decided that he wanted to be an attorney. He went from elementary school at East Hill Christian to Washington High School, which was a public school. I was concerned if Isaac would match up with the other students at a public high school, but sure enough, he did. He actually graduated with a 4.2 GPA and I was proud of him for that. He worked hard. I really have to give credit to my wife. She would encourage Isaac to do his homework. She would let him play a little bit when he came home from school, but then made sure that every day he did his homework.

I'll never forget one day when he came home from grade school crying because he had made a B grade. He really wanted to make A's. I didn't put any pressure on him. I had always told my boys to learn so that they know something not for the grade, but so that they knew the subject and it would stick with them.

Isaac went on to Florida State University and then Coastal Law School and he was on the Law Review there. That's a high honor only for those who make good grades and were honorable.

When he went to Florida State University, he wanted to be in a fraternity. He said, "Dad, I know I'm a Christian, and I want to be a Christian, but I want to experience the full college experience."

I was worried about him because he wasn't going to church on a regular basis. I thought it would be good if we could do a pilgrimage. The type of pilgrimage I had in mind meant we would travel somewhere together to experience a spiritual refreshing. It needed to be one where everyone involved (Debbie, Isaac and I) would have something that we each liked about it.

Now my wife, Debbie, loves the prophetic. She loves going to church meetings where the speaker is gifted prophetically. So, as I was thinking about this pilgrimage, I thought how much Debbie loves the prophetic. I remembered there was a group under Rick Joyner that's called Morningstar Church, which is a prophetic church. It's really not a denomination but a group of people that love the prophetic. Rick Joyner operates in the prophetic and the people on his team operate in the prophetic. They relate to other prophetic churches. They train people in the prophetic and have prophetic conferences. Their music is prophetic and they worship until they can get into the presence of the Lord. I thought a trip there would be perfect for Debbie. Ok one down, three to go.

Their music is very unusual..... It's a bunch of guys who are young and have long hair and play all sorts of instruments and their sound is different and I just knew that Isaac would like their music. Two down, one to go.

So I thought we would take a pilgrimage to Charlotte,

North Carolina, to a Morningstar prophetic conference. I didn't know who the main speaker was going to be, but I hoped I would like the conference. I'm not necessarily attracted to the prophetic like Debbie is, but I know the Lord has used me prophetically sometimes with prophetic dreams and sometimes He'll show me some things about somebody. So, I hoped I would like the conference.

I also previously told Debbie that I had been reading some things by a man named John Paul Jackson and I told Debbie that if Brother Jackson was anywhere nearby I wanted to go to one of his services. He intrigued me with some of his teaching and preaching. I read about his call and he had a really neat testimony. Come to find out, he was the main speaker at the Morningstar conference. That night when we got there, we found out that his main topic was going to be "Divine Justice". Three out of three, "Confirmation." It was a very unusual sermon on Divine Justice. By the way, I loved it.

Debbie loved this whole idea because we were going to be picking up Isaac. He had been away at school and she had been missing him and we were going to be all together. Well, Isaac flew to Charlotte from Tallahassee and we flew to Charlotte from Pensacola and we met there. The service was great, and I just loved the preaching and teaching.

One of the things that happened the next day at the conference was that we were given an appointed time to meet with a group of their people who had prophetic gifting. They inquire of the Lord and try to hear a word from the Lord for you. They are trained that a prophetic word needs to be edification, exhortation or comfort. We went into this big gymnasium type place where they have a school called Creative Release.

Many of the young people that are in that church go to this school. One of the interesting things they do is when the preacher is speaking, they have a couple of people drawing and doing paintings of what their impression is of what they think the Lord is saying in the service. Then they have all these neat works of art sculptures and pottery and all kinds of different things that they make in school. They ask the Holy Spirit to help release their gifting. Get it? Creative Release. I love it.

So we went into this big gymnasium and they had modules with partitions. There were three people that were going to minister to the three of us, Debbie, Isaac and me. We sat down and they sat across from us and we said our first names and they said their first names and then we began to pray.

Isaac was in the middle, and the girl that was straight across from him was beautiful. She was a young blonde about Isaac's age, and all of a sudden, she began to cry these big tears and she said, "Oh, Isaac! We need you in the body of Christ! The Lord shows me plainly that you love justice!" Debbie and Isaac and I just about fell out of our chairs. We couldn't believe that she said that the first thing. She said, "You're not given to sensationalism and you see so much of what's false in the church and we need your discernment! We need you, Isaac!" It was great and we all cried. They said other words to the rest of us that were good, but I'm telling you, Isaac loves justice.

During another teaching session that we attended in the main sanctuary, they were teaching on the prophetic and they would have times when you would try to learn how to hear from the Lord. They would have exercises where you would try to do just that—"hear from the Lord."

They broke us up in groups of five. Debbie and Isaac split from me to join other groups. Then we began these exercises among our groups. The last exercise, we stood in our group, closed our eyes, and tried to hear a word or see a picture in our mind. Then we had to figure out which person the word was for in the group. I was only receiving a little bit, but when the speaker said to pray to see a picture, Isaac saw a holographic picture in his mind. It looked like a line drawing in 3-D of a tiger's face. Suddenly the tiger's face went straight out in front of him in three-D and living color. He was staring straight into a tiger's eyes. The leader of the whole class then said, "Whatever you have seen or heard is for you!" It just showed me that somehow Isaac is gifted in those ways. Yes, a tiger describes him. That, to me was so cool. However, probably the most confirming thing of the whole trip was when the young girl said, "Isaac loves justice".

Today, Isaac is an attorney. Just out of law school he wanted to work for the public defender's office. He wanted experience going to trial by jury. Many people might think that you should become a prosecutor if you love justice. But Isaac said no, that if there was one person that's innocent and doesn't have the money and needs a good attorney to have justice that he wanted to be there for them. Now he is a partner in his own criminal law practice. And that's what he does; seek justice for each one of his clients. He told me when he stands before the jury, he feels the anointing of the Lord. I once asked him, "What if the person is guilty?" He said, "Dad, I work for God and the constitution!" He said, "I need to follow my heart and ask the Lord and seek justice, love justice and pursue justice and the Lord will help bring it about."

"Isaac Loves Justice"

Chapter Thirty-Four

"My Dad: Bigger than Life"

I know you've probably heard it said before that sometimes a man or woman's dad can have an impression on them that's bigger than reality. That was definitely the case with my Dad. Actually, I think he earned every bit of that impression, because I knew him and saw him do things that other people never saw him do. This may not be as interesting to people outside the family, but to the grandkids, great grandkids, or great-great grandkids, it might be interesting to know about him.

Simply stated, his character was bigger than life.

The reason I say he was bigger than life is that he gave that impression to many people. I never saw or heard him cheat, lie, or steal. He was a man of his word. His word was his bond. You could absolutely trust him. He was a man of integrity. He was a man of character.

He was the only man that I ever knew that other men feared. He worked about two hundred people at his rock quarry, where he was the general manager and president. He had a No Fraternization Policy. His employees were not his friends. To me this policy was bitter-sweet. I knew my management style would not be that way.

Fraternization, if I understand it right, is where somebody will discuss or talk about their own feelings to become friends with employees. There's a principle I've heard said, "Familiarity breeds contempt." It means if you get too familiar, they don't respect you. He never showed others his weakness. No foolishness, only his hasty, scary strength.

My dad wasn't a giant man, but he was a big man; he was six feet tall and he weighed 230. He had a big head, a big set of shoulders, and a big chest, so that made him seem larger than life.

Another thing that made him seem larger than life is that he was strongly opinionated. Just about everyone would rather agree with him than disagree because his attitude toward his opinion was an unspoken "I'm right, don't disagree." Most of the time I would relate to him by saying what I knew he wanted to hear. So, I had and wanted to keep his favor. But many times, as his son, I would disagree silently.

One subject where I disagreed was on environmental issues. He was a coal miner back in West Virginia and Ohio. Then in Florida, he had a rock quarry, and he also loved being a timber man. He had a saying, "No one can tell me what to do in my own backyard. If I want to dig a hole, I can dig a hole." The word environmentalist would almost make him want to spit. He definitely didn't like governmental control.

I grew up in a different generation; I grew up in the sixties. I was born in 1951, so in the sixties I was a teenager. I began to question authority, I love thinking that I was an environmental minded man because it made sense!

My point is we have a small planet that has boundaries, and if we pollute it, it is just wrong. Things like dumping the waste from New York City into the ocean just really appalled me and does to this day. This is one area that my Dad and I had a large disagreement. I once told him that if you were in your bathtub and I dumped just a spoonful of garbage into your tub, it would pollute that bathtub. You would be angry because it would be so wrong. He saw my point. He couldn't understand me being an environmentalist though. I wouldn't really argue with him about that. He was such a strong, opinionated man. I loved him anyway. I have always tried to honor him.

He was also somewhat angry. Even as I tell these stories about him to his and my heritage, I don't, in any way, want to disparage him. I would never want to make him look bad. I don't even want to tell negative things about him, because in my mind he was this GREAT man with a big giant heart.

I don't want to pass on to my heritage anger and harshness, however, I once thought I had to be harsh to prove I was a man and please my dad. When I became a true Christian, I changed my mind about a lot of things. I found out that I could be strong and have no fear but still be gentle. The Word says, "Let your gentle spirit [your graciousness, unselfishness, mercy, tolerance, and patience] be known to all people. The Lord is near." Philippians 4:5 AMP

I saw over and over where men would come to him in need, especially at the rock plant, and he would help them. One time a guy came to him who owed him a debt for the rock that he had gotten for some sort of construction-type work. I remember the man came into our living room and talked to my dad. I was a boy, and it was one of the first times I saw a grown man cry. He cried before my dad and said, "Please, I'm not trying to not pay you for this debt. I just don't have the money, Mr. Newlin." He offered to sell my dad his land that he had for fifty dollars an acre, and now it's worth fifty thousand an acre.

But my dad felt like that would be taking advantage of him, so he said, "Is there anything you can do that you can make a payment with?"

The man said, "I don't have it."
My dad said, "Keep working hard, we'll work it out, you can pay me as you can." The man did pay him over time. I just saw him have a big heart toward different individuals. For some men, it was like they would die for him.

As I said though, he didn't really share his feelings with other men. Somehow that made them respect him, because they never saw the weak side. When somebody runs their mouth too much, people don't respect that. They like somebody that's together with their thoughts and few with their words. The Bible says if you'll not speak, but just listen, people will think you're wise. I saw over and over where men were afraid of him. They all called him Mr. Newlin. Even the older men called him Mr. Newlin. Some of that he earned from his positions. He was the president of West Coast Rock Company. He was the president of the Rod and Gun Club, and he was the president of Cypress Lake Country Club.

He always wore a hat. I never saw my dad without a hat unless he was at the dinner table or the supper table. I think he got that from his granddad, who had a large farm. My dad said he had never seen his grandfather without his hat except at the dinner table. My dad was going bald, so maybe that had something to do with it, but he loved his hats. He mostly wore big straw hats.

He would be known as Mr. Newlin. He expected it. He had an air about him. Part of it was because he was quick to act. I saw this a number of times, and the men saw it. They had heard stories.

One example of him being a little bit scary and hasty occurred with a guy named Gator Man. Gator Man was a tough hombre from Immokalee, Florida. He was wiry and kind of big. He was countrified, and very proud. Kind of good-looking, and he was a great diesel mechanic, the best in the shop. This Gator Man was the real deal. He is who Bert Reynolds tried to act like in the movie "Gator McCluskie". Gator Man was definitely the coolest guy working at the rock quarry.

One day, Gator Man had made a rare mistake and he had messed up an engine. He had been coming in late and drinking some. So, my dad told Bud, the manager under my dad at that time, to fire him. Bud said something to Gator Man, and Gator Man made out like he was going to cut Bud. Gator Man had a reputation that when he fought, he would cut you with his blade, that is his sharp knife. Bud was a big guy, but he went flying off in his truck because he thought better than to get into it with Gator Man.

Well, Bud went to the quarry office and told my dad what Gator Man said and did. He told Bud to stay at the office. So, here comes my dad, roaring up in a cloud of dust in his big ol' Olds 98. When my Dad got out and came into the shop, Gator Man was standing there waiting on him.
My Dad said, "Gator Man you been drinking again?"
Yes," replied Gator Man.

My dad said, "You're fired. Go to the office and get your check." Gator Man made a rush toward my dad. Just at that time, my dad picked up a crescent wrench, a big one, and made a rush at Gator Man.

Just before my dad hit Gator Man in the side of the head with the wrench, Gator Man backed up. They looked each other in the eyes. He knew and everyone else in the shop knew he was one second away from eternity!
He said, "I like you, Mr. Newlin and I like working here!"
My dad said, " Get your check!"
Gator man got his stuff and he left. But it was so close to horrible violence happening in that shop. The point was, the men saw it. Gator Man was one tough dude, but when he made a move at my old man, my old man made a move at him.
When my dad got back to the quarry office, he said to Bud, "You're fired. If you can't handle something like that you can't be boss."
The legend of John M. Newlin went up a notch at that day.

That's the way I saw him my whole life. Especially with livestock, he would be real quick to move. I remember we had this one young horse that was just acting crazy in a stall. Rather than be afraid of him like I was, I saw my dad jump right in the stall with him and grab that horse by the halter around his head and just shook it. He said something very loudly, "Come up out of there, you son of a bitch!" The way he said it, the horse paid attention, and everyone who was listening paid attention, and the horse stood at attention. It was that quick, hasty, scary action that probably made such an impression on me.

My dad would take me hunting and fishing, even at an

early age. I'll never forget, as a boy of about six, we would go to a place called Ten Mile Creek. We used cane poles and a bobber, and there was just something about seeing that bobber go under. I would lift up that pole and get that fish on. It was just marvelous to me. I didn't want to stop. I've used the expression many times when someone says something about fishing: "Yeah, my dad had to spank me to quit." I've often said I loved to fish even if I didn't have a hook. I just loved to fish and hunt with him.

My dad never bragged. He never really talked much about what happened to him in the past. There were things I wished he would tell me about. One reason why I'm doing this book is to tell you about him, and to tell about myself to my great grandkids.

He fought in World War II in a place called Guadalcanal. It must have been a horrible battle. He was in the Seabees, which is a branch of the Navy. The Seabees would go in and put the landing places for the Marines. Sometimes they would go in ahead of the Marines. But he would hardly ever talk about it. I read a newspaper clipping that his mother (my grandmother) had saved out of the hometown paper. There were 250 Seabees in his group, and only 50 survived. He had said one time that his best buddy had gotten killed in a Jeep right next to him. Many times, he'd be running his bulldozer and snipers would be pinging bullets off of it. He would run a dozer and have a rifle next to him at the same time.

I think that World War II experience really changed him. It made him look at life differently. I'm not sure whether I would say it changed him for the good or the bad. I believe he suffered from undiagnosed P.T.S.D. (Post Traumatic Stress

Disorder). In some ways it was very hard on him; in other ways I think it made him into the unusual individual that he was. He did say that he would read Psalm 91 and pray and believe Psalm 91. Psalm 91 speaks of "no evil will come nigh you. Many will die on your left hand or your right hand, but none will get you." That psalm had a really big meaning in his life.

He also said that he would be in a foxhole that they had dug, on an island. When the Japanese bombs would hit the island and he was in the foxhole, the land would quiver and shake. Some of the older men would totally lose their minds and have a nervous breakdown from the bombs hitting.

One time he got up out of the foxhole, and a Japanese Zero airplane had been hit with some shells and was smoking and burning and crashing. It flew right over his head and crashed right behind him. He said that he had an epiphany, where he felt that when it was your time to die, you would die. Since that plane had not hit him and exploded so close to him, it changed his outlook on dying, and about fear.

He also played football at Ohio State. He went to Ohio State University and majored in Animal Husbandry. As I've said many times, he could look at an animal and tell if it had a good confirmation, or good lines and features for that kind of animal.

At Ohio State, he played both ways. He played offense and defensive end. I also read in a newspaper article, that when he was in high school, with equipment on, that he could run the 100-yard dash in 10 seconds flat. That is pretty amazing, because when I was in high school, our track star (the person who ran the 100-yard dash) ran it in 10 seconds flat with track shoes on and no equipment. These days they run the 100- meter, but he would run 100 yards in 10 seconds flat.

This is a story illustrating my dad's strength. I'd like to say and think that he didn't ever know his own strength. He never worked out with weights that I know of. He would ball up the muscles in his arms and flex his biceps, and I swear it was like a full, big, hard softball as bicep muscles.

We had six or eight different cattle leases, and we had what we called woods cattle. In one of our cow pastures the owner drilled an oil well. This wasn't our oil well; this was a leased pasture. We leased the cattle rights. Because it was a dry well, they tore it all down, however, they left a 55-gallon drum of gear oil. It was full and had never been opened. I'm not sure why they left it there.

So, we decided that rather than just let it rust out there in the open, we would pick it up and use it. This was after a period of time of six months. So, we decided we were going to put it in the back of our pickup truck. We got out and saw that it was full. We always drove a four-wheel drive Ford, and it was a little bit jacked up. That means it was raised up a little bit on a lift and had big tires.

So, our truck was jacked up pretty high, which meant the tailgate was pretty high. Trying to put a 55-gallon drum full of oil in the back of the truck required a fairly high lift. In fact, a 55-gallon drum full of oil weighs somewhere close to 440 pounds.

So the two of us picked up the drum and set it in the back of the truck. What amazed me was that I didn't pick up that much. I just couldn't believe that we picked it up that easily and set it in the back of the truck. So, what that's saying is, my dad is the one who picked up that drum of oil. It just showed me once again, that was My Dad: Bigger Than Life.

In conclusion, at one time after he died, I was really wondering if my Dad was in heaven. If you asked anybody in my family if they thought he was in heaven, they would all say yes, because he had such a big heart. I'm not sure that's the Lord's only criteria. I was more than a little disturbed thinking on this subject. So, I looked to heaven and asked my Heavenly Father if my Dad was saved and in heaven.

I didn't hear the answer right then. But that night, I had a vivid God Dream. In the dream, a large Angel dressed in shining white stood on a hill and shouted to me, "John, your Dad says he's waiting on you!" That gave me peace! So maybe even to the Angels my dad is bigger than life. He will always be to me.

I have tried to and will continue to live obedient to the scripture; "Honor Your Father..." Ex. 20:12 KJV

Conclusion

     This is the conclusion to my **book** of stories. To help you understand the purpose of this book, I will quote A.W. Tozer. "God formed us for Himself. The ancient questions are what and why?" And he answers them in one short sentence hardly matched in any uninspired work.

Question: "What is the chief end of man?

Answer: "Man's chief end is to glorify God and enjoy Him forever."

     Dear readers, my hope and **purpose** of this book is that God would put His spark in you and light His fire of faith. This is my conclusion. Fear Him, hear Him and obey Him. Call out to Jesus and you will come to realize the story God has put in you.

Made in the USA
Lexington, KY
16 November 2019